Blazes & Brimstone

Gruenberg, Linda.
    Blazes & Brimstone / Linda Gruenberg.

ISBN: 978-91-986317-3-9

Copyright © 2022 by Linda Gruenberg

All rights reserved. No part of this work may be reproduced or transmitted in any form or by any means, electronic or mechanical, including photocopying and recording, or by any information storage or retrieval system, except as may be expressly permitted by the 1976 Copyright Act or in writing from the author.

Imprint: Kenda Press

www.kendapress.com

www.lindagruenberg.com

Blazes & Brimstone

Linda Gruenberg

Kenda Press
2022

For my mother, again.
She is a breath of fresh air and energy. Everyone I
know wants to be like her, including me.

Look for these other titles by Linda Gruenberg:

Hummer
Good Luck Chestnut
The Isa Book 1
The Isa Book 2
The Isa Book 3
The Isa Book 4

Read more about the author at:
www.lindagruenberg.com

Foreword, or Mrs. O'Leary's Cow

Many of you know the song about Mrs. O'Leary's cow, right? If you're like me, the tune and rhythm catch in your head as soon as you hear **"One Dark Night."**

One dark night, when we were all in bed,
Mrs. O'Leary took the lantern to the shed,
And when the cow kicked it over,
she winked her eye and said,
It'll be a hot time in the old town tonight.

But did you know that the Old Town in the song is Chicago? And that Mrs. O'Leary and her cow became scapegoats for a fire that went down in history as the "Great Chicago Fire?" The slander against the O'Leary family turned out to be just that—slander. One hundred years after Mrs. O'Leary's death, the Chicago City Council officially absolved her of blame by presenting a gold-stamped certificate to her family. The song went down in history, but few know about the gold stamp.

So, what does Mrs. O'Leary's innocent cow have to do with the fire in Holland, Michigan, which this book, *Blazes & Brimstone,* is about? It happened the same day, that's what. And Holland wasn't the only small city that burned that day. Three towns in Michigan (Holland, Manistee and Port Huron), and one town in Wisconsin (Peshtigo) also had terrible fires the exact same time. Coincidence? It makes you wonder what was going on with cows that night, kicking over all those lanterns, right?

    Chicago with its population of just over 334,000 had 300 deaths, and one-third of the city's population was left homeless. Holland with its population of about 3,000, lost all its city area except, wondrously, Hope Preparatory School which would become Hope College, but there was only one death. Peshtigo's fire was by far the most horrific. Peshtigo, with its population of only 1,700, lost between 1,200 to 2,400 people. This death toll includes surrounding areas and is such a wide estimate because local records were also destroyed in the fire. Nobody knows the real number. With the flow of pioneers, loggers, gold diggers, and other groups moving between Michigan's Upper Peninsula and the West, the number of unknown people caught in the 1.2-million-acre fire is impossible to calculate. Sadly, many people who didn't burn in the fire drowned in wells or died of hypothermia in the cold water where they tried to escape to survive.

    So, what really started the great and terrible fires in Illinois, Wisconsin, and Michigan on October 8th, 1871?

    There's a theory that a meteorite shower hit the Great Lakes region that night, that a fragment of Biela's Comet broke off, causing spontaneous ignitions in the entire region surrounding Lake Michigan. The meteorite shower would explain the tornadoes of flame that people described. There were reports of falling "fire balloons" and rising "fire devils," or convection spirals that spit burning debris to spread the fire across rivers and plowed fields. It would also explain why the fires were simultaneous, widespread, yet disconnected from each other.

On the other hand, some claim that the logging practices of the time didn't need a lot of help to fan fire into flames. There were controlled—or not so controlled—burns already smoldering here and there after areas of virgin forest had been cut. Some farmers also reportedly burned fields. The autumn had already been in drought status for weeks or months. On October 8, 1871, extraordinarily high winds were also widespread. With controversial logging methods and the addition of high winds, no other cause was likely needed.

This novel, *Blazes & Brimstone,* tells the story of just one of those fires: the one in Holland, Michigan. And why did I write it? Why just Holland? Why horses? Why just children and a livery stable? All because, as a Hope College student, I caught sight of a small pump organ in the Holland Museum. The organ had been buried to survive the fire, dug up again, and saved. There was a Bible in the museum too: a Dutch-language Bible with some scorched pages but otherwise spared.

These artifacts caught my imagination and pulled me back into history to find out things:
- Why did they bury the organ?
- Who all lived in Holland, Michigan other than the Dutch?
- Were there any past slaves or free black people who had always been free?
- What about the Native Americans, and which tribes?
- What if there were pregnant women escaping the fire, and what would that have been like?

Finding the answers took me to libraries, museums, and websites. I found out that there were the "Americans"—what Hollanders called anyone who wasn't Dutch and had been in the New World longer. The Ottawa, a native tribe, had roots in the area but spent much of their time up north, so weren't present at the time of the fire. There may have been both the black early freedom seekers and past slaves, but not many. The Underground Railroad route ran further east, going through Detroit and into Canada.

I have gathered a group of all these people on the pages of *Blazes & Brimstone* to reflect what could have been. Why horses? Because I surround myself with horses just for the happiness of it.

With that leap from the known into the possible, I do my best to tell the truth of what I've learned. We've all heard the term "melting pot" to describe how nationalities mixed together in America. It's still happening, of course. Tragedies and natural disasters are still happening, too, and the same tragedies that tear people apart bring others together, often moving them from narrow to wide, from closed to accepting, from neighborhoods of one color, to friends of many colors. It's beautiful how that can happen.

Here I am at the end of my introduction, and I still have Mrs. O'Leary's song in my head. I don't know if you have ever heard the backwards version, but if not, you might like this:

One dark bed, when we were all in night.
Mrs. O'Leary took the shed out to the light,
And when the kick cowed it over,
She eyed her wink and said
It'll be a hot town in the old time tonight.

Dutch guide to Pronunciations

"*Ja*" means "yeah" and is pronounced **Yah**.

Nee means "no" and is pronounced **Nay**.

Dank u is "Thank you," pronounced **donk ooh**.

Dank u zeer is "Thank you very much," pronounced **donk ooh zeer**.

Dank God is "thank God," as you can see.

Hallo is "hello," pronounced almost the same as **hello**.

Voor de lol means "For the fun of it" pronounced like it looks.

De stad means "the city," pronounced **de stahd**.

Goede means "good," pronounced **Goodeh**.

Goede Morgon means "good morning," pronounced **Goodeh morgon**.

Mevrouw is Mrs., pronounced **Mefrow**.

Het regend is "It's raining," pronounced **Hate raygand**.

Dank u zeer for reading!

Blazes & Brimstone

ONE

October 8, 1871, Holland, Michigan

Brimstone

For most of his life, Lyle Hemmis figured he was going to Hell. Usually that didn't bother him much because, though he definitely believed in Hell, he didn't really believe in dying. At least he didn't think it would ever happen to him. But today was different. Today for the first time he thought he might die. And soon.

The church pew was hard and narrow beneath him, the psalter hymn book heavy in his lap. His older brother, Rudy, was warm on one side and his father warm on the other. The dominie—or preacher, as the Americans called him—prayed in low, gurgling, singsong Dutch for rain and to escape the burning flames of Hell's fire—or the real fire, Lyle wasn't sure which.

Lyle had his eyes closed, but all he could think about was the smoke. His eyes hurt. All week long, the smell and the drifting soot from the forest fire had burned inside his nose and reddened the rims of his eyelids. Right now, when the smoke was especially grey and thick, he didn't know what to worry about more: the smoke, Winny having the baby, or about the whole city burning?

The dominie's favorite subject was Hell. He described it in ways that made the hair on Lyle's arms crawl. The dominie made it seem like Hell was just outside the church doorway, right on the front stoop—along with some vile insects, too, most likely.

"Nobody believes in Hell more than the Dutch," his stepmother, Winny, had said once. Winny was American, so she was free to make little comments like that.

Lyle could smell the brimstone—or something just like it: an acrid smoky smell that hurt. It gave Lyle a sickening feeling, like somebody had reached into his rib cage and clamped hold of his heart. He was carrying around a tight, buzzing place in his chest and had to squeeze his breath past it.

The dominie wasn't done praying yet, but Lyle's eyes sprang open anyway. Even though it was only three o'clock in the afternoon, the candles were all lit as if it were night, and Lyle had to squint to see through the smoky candlelight.

Lyle looked across to the women's side of the church to see Winny and his little sister, Aggie. Aggie was slouched over sideways, resting her head on Winny's extended belly. Winny's eyes were closed, her face angled toward the ceiling and catching some of the gold candlelight across one cheekbone and her soft mouth. Her hand moved gently in Aggie's hair.

Lyle squinted to see if the signs of her pains were on Winny's face. Twice today she'd stopped to put both hands on her stomach. His father had asked her if these were the pains, and she said they didn't really hurt. She could come to church.

Lyle tried not to think of his real mother, but there she was anyway, floating in front of his eyes like all the smoke. She and a tiny baby were in the same coffin, swirling gently just out of Lyle's reach. It was the baby Lyle had nagged his mother to have, all just so he could have a new little brother or sister.

The thought of Winny in a coffin with a baby made him suck in his breath.

Rudy pulled Lyle's arm to show him what he was doing—twisting around so far and staring.

"Turn around," he whispered and slid his fingers through his sandy-blond hair. His broad, freckled face made his nose look thin and small, and he pulled it before he added, "She'll be okay."

But of course, Rudy couldn't know that.

Dominie VandePol finally stretched his arms out wide, hands down, getting close to the "Amen," Lyle hoped.

"As the great theologian said," the dominie prayed, "God, you hold us over the pit of hell, much as one holds a spider or some loathsome insect over the fire."

The dominie left a pause for the squirming of the loathsome insect to fill. Then he continued.

"Spare us from your looming judgment. Teach our hearts repentance and spare us the lash of your flaming rod of judgment."

Lyle shuddered and peeked through one eye to see if the prayer might be almost over. He saw deacon Jenema with a long feather tickler reach into the center of the pew in front of him to wake up one of the old uncles. How could anyone sleep through that? Lyle wondered. Lyle glanced at Rudy again whose mouth twitched into a one-sided smile when the old man waved the feather away from his nose and jerked awake. When their eyes met, Lyle squeezed his eyes shut again.

"We are sinners who deserve Hell and Brimstone, but we pray for your mercy to hold us above the flames."

Lyle peaked again to see if the deacon with the feather tickler had found any more victims, but he stood alert watching the dominie this time. Maybe he was also longing for the end of the prayer.

"Merciful God. You hold us by the slenderest of threads, yet you hold us. Keep us above the flames. Turn our wicked hearts to you."

Lyle felt the end coming.

"In the name of the Father, the Son, and the Holy Ghost. Amen."

At last.

Now others in the church came alive, eyes opening, looking around again. Lyle wondered if anyone else's skin was crawling with the thought of the scorched spiders or if it was just him with his guilty conscience.

Lyle saw Winny's face twitch. He stared at her, but all she did was lift her handkerchief and sneeze discreetly into it. The smoke was getting to her. Lyle's eyes stung, too. If the fire were as small as everyone kept saying, he didn't see how it could make the sky so dark or make so many ashes fall. The farmers around the edge of *de stad*, as they called the town of Holland, had been plowing strips along the forest edge to keep the fire from leaping across. The Eagle Fire Company had been at work, too, watering down the buildings closest to the fire.

Lyle felt his father's hand descend on his fist. It was cold and heavy. Lyle looked up, saw his father's mouth sucked down at the corners, and with sudden shock of memory he returned, once again, to his mother's funeral. It was as if his father had shown that same face only once before, when Lyle's own mother lay in her coffin, but ever since had carefully schooled it out of his features. But today he couldn't help himself, Lyle thought. Was it because Winny would die, too, having her baby? Or because the fire was going to come sweeping over them all?

Did his father know that it was Lyle who had wished so hard for another little baby sibling and even nagged his mother about it?

A loud noise made Lyle jump. When he looked around to see where the noise had come from, Rudy gestured at the open window. The flag outside was cracking so loudly that Dominie VandePol stopped mid-sentence. Everyone in the church seemed to notice the wind change. One moment things had been still and smoky, and the next, the air swirled and lifted the pages of the open pulpit Bible.

A distant church bell began ringing.

Lyle heard gasping and murmuring from up and down the aisle.

The flag was still snapping when Dominie VandePol raised his voice, found his place in the catechism, and started working back into his rhythm. But when a second distant church added its tolling to the first, Deacon Jenema walked right across the front of the church to the window. He looked at the dominie and the dominie looked back at him. Then the piercing whistle of the Cappon & Bertsch Tannery blew as if it were quitting time, as if this weren't Sunday, but any weekday, and Lyle felt tingles across his scalp.

It was the call for the Eagle Fire Company to send out the horses.

"The fire broke through," Deacon Jenema said, and Dominie VandePol didn't even give the benediction.

"They're going to need help," he said and made sweeping motions with his arms toward the door. Suddenly, everyone was standing up as if to sing a hymn, waiting to get into the aisle.

"Which way is the wind from?" someone called out.

"Southwest," someone answered back.

"Graafschap is in trouble, then."

Lyle felt his stomach go cold with chills. He had cousins in Graafschap. And if Graafschap was in trouble, so was Holland.

"Go with God," somebody said.

"Go with God, go with God," Lyle heard coming from all over the church. His father and Winny met in the aisle and whispered hurriedly together. Father's face had returned to its normal look of concern and control. He always knew what to do, and he knew what to do even now.

Aggie gave Lyle's arm a yank, so he'd bend his head down to listen to her.

"Dominie VandePol shouldn't smoke so many cigars before church," she whispered. "It smokes up the whole place!" Aggie's hair was yellow-blond, whiter on top so that when Winny pulled it back into a braid, the braid looked like a white and yellow ear of corn. Her mouth was small and always pink, and she had a way of looking sideways before she laughed. She looked sideways now, then giggled.

"Hey!" Lyle said. "It's not funny anymore." She had made the same joke the week before. "Don't you know this is serious?" Still, he couldn't help smiling into her smiling face.

"Lyle," Father said, "You run home and get that mare hitched up to the surrey." He said it as calmly, like there wasn't a fire in Graafschap. He always used the word run. Run down to the cellar for some potatoes. Run over to Widow Reis with the news. Now, run home and hitch up the mare. Then he added, "Winny will be along shortly."

Aggie pulled on his sleeve again and pretended to puff on a cigar. Her eyes slid all the way sideways, as if she were about to burst.

"Quit it," Lyle said, but not seriously. He gave her hand a squeeze, ducked out of the church door and ran past Rudy down the stone steps.

It felt good to run away from the smoky church, the thought of spiders, and even away from Winny and her big belly. He pumped his legs as fast as he could. He veered around a black and white dog biting itself, then skipped lightly across a stone curb before he raced home down Market Street. The smoke was hard to breathe, but he kept running, panting and feeling his lungs burn, right on past the saddle maker's store and the portrait gallery, past his friend Pieter's house, then through the widow Reis' back yard and into his own yard next to the livery stable. He couldn't see the yellow of fire anywhere, but the sky was dark, and the smoke blew in swirls around him. Dry leaves scuttled along the ground or flew up in sudden whirlwinds. A clothesline snapped.

He wondered how far away Hell was. Dominie VandePol never seemed to say. Lyle shivered.

TWO

Blazes

Lyle burst into the barn, and Cookie nickered at the sound of the slamming door.

"Just me," Lyle announced, gasping for breath. Cookie pushed against her stall door. Lyle gave Red, a small chestnut mare, a pat, then slid a hand along Cookie's neck, under the warmth of her baby-short mane.

"How you doing, pretty?" he said to her.

"Miss your mama?" He could just make out the white cookie shape on her forehead in the dim light. The cookie marking was how she got her name. *Koekje* was the Dutch word for cookie, and it sounded almost the same as English. Cookie rested her jaw on Lyle's shoulder and then wiggled her muzzle against his ear. It tickled.

He pressed his nose into the soft side of her face, the soft part where her skin was velvet, and he felt himself smile into her warm breath.

This was Cookie's first full day of being weaned. Their next-door neighbor, Mr. Boone, the livery man with only one hand, had traded horses with them to help with the weaning. Mr. Boone kept

Cookie's mother, Scarlet, at his place, while Red was here instead.

Red would pull the surrey and keep Cookie company, but so far, Cookie didn't seem to think much of the arrangement. Neither did Lyle, for that matter. Scarlet and Cookie were his favorite horses in the world. He had watched Scarlet give birth to Cookie, and he'd been the one to clear the slippery birth sack from Cookie's nostrils. Scarlet's licking tongue also found Lyle, slicking his hair up. It made Scarlet almost his own mother, and Cookie, his own baby.

Scarlet and Red both had white blazes down the face, just like half the horses in Mr. Boone's livery stable.

Father had been saying for weeks that it was high time to get those two horses independent. He was tired of working around Cookie's feedings. A sewing machine repairman sometimes had to travel quite far in a day, especially a repairman with as widespread a reputation as Mr. Hemmis had.

"I don't see why Scarlet has to go to Mr. Boone's, though," Lyle had protested. Surely there were other places.

"He stamps at us," Aggie had added. It was true. Mr. Boone never let any kids near his horses. If they stepped up to a horse that was stopped in front of his yard, for instance, he'd stamp the floor of his carriage. Or if he were on his porch, and they slowed down passing his house, he'd stamp the wooden floor of his porch: bang, bang, bang as if he were shooing away a dog. Lyle thought he looked something like a hound, too, the way his cheeks and the pouches under his eyes sagged downward. "Scram," he might yell if he said anything at all. Then he'd chuckle when they went running. He liked shaking the hook of his left hand at them.

At school, the kids explained to each other that Mr. Boone got his hand run over by a train. His boot got caught in the railroad ties, so he couldn't get away in time. The train ran over his hand. Sliced it right off. Lyle and his friend Pieter sometimes played on the tracks, pretending to be Mr. Boone getting their hands cut off.

"Maybe he seems mean to kids," his father had said, "but he treats his horses well enough."

"Mr. Boone will rent her out, though," Lyle said. He didn't like the idea of strangers driving Scarlet.

"Well, sure he will," his father said. "That's part of the arrangement."

Lyle had to sigh. He knew that his father was right. The horses next door were well taken care of, with gleaming coats and muscles that rippled as they moved.

Now Lyle grabbed the water bucket. Cookie slurped hastily down to the spongy wooden bottom of the bucket, so he had to pump more water for her. He didn't know if all the whinnying had made her so thirsty or if it was the smoke.

When both horses had drunk, Lyle led Red out of the stall.

"Come on, girl. Time to go to work. It's not wrong to work on a Sunday if it's an emergency."

He threw the harness over her back, then realized that each piece was going to need readjusting—the collar tightened, the belly band tightened, the breeching raised up higher around her rump. Lyle tore at the buckles, trying to get the heavy leather out of the keepers. Even Scarlet's harness didn't like this arrangement, Lyle thought. He snugged the collar around Red's neck and fit the hames into it.

The surrey was a two-seater, and though both the seats had faced forward under the canopy at one time, Father had changed the back seat. He had unbolted it and flipped it backwards, so he had more room for transporting sewing machines between seats. Now the canopy covered only the front, and the children rode facing back, their seat extending past the back wheels. Father had even built a step halfway down for Aggie, though she just leapt over it like Lyle and Rudy did.

Lyle led Red over one shaft then backed her smoothly into place. Winny caught up, breathing hard and holding Aggie by the hand. Their skirts blew wildly in the wind; their hair flew in wisps across their faces.

"Good job," Winny said, surprising Lyle by fervently kissing his cheek. She smelled like roses.

"If Graafschap is burning, Aunt Reka and Uncle Bernard and the kids will need a place to stay. I'm going to look for them—meet them, I hope," she added. She gave a little shiver, imagining the cousins' house burned down, Lyle thought. Or she was imagining that their cousins were themselves in danger, and that's why she kissed him so thankfully. Even now she squeezed her eyes shut a moment and her lips moved.

"Let Uncle Bernard and Aunt Reka and Jenny and Sietze be okay," Lyle said quickly under his breath, in a prayer of his own, because he knew that was what Winny was doing—praying. "And us, too," he added.

"Where is Father?" Lyle asked as he twisted the tugs of the harness over the eye hooks. "And Rudy?"

"They're heading for the fire," she said. "All the men are. I want you to stay here to watch Aggie."

Men, she'd said, referring to Rudy. It seemed crazy to think of his big freckle-faced brother as a man. Even Rudy would have joked around if he'd overheard it—given a formal bow or something, keeping a straight face until the last possible second, and then the corners of his lips turning up to let Lyle know it was all a big joke. Lyle wondered if he'd be able to keep a straight face when he was fourteen like Rudy. Somehow, he didn't think so. At eleven, he could wiggle either eyebrow separately and his ears together, but he couldn't keep a straight face. Aggie, at five, could crack jokes when she ought to be scared, but Lyle didn't know if this was the same talent or not.

"Why can't we come?" Aggie asked.

"There's not room," Winny answered. "If I find them. They'll have a lot of things if…" her voice trailed off, then she gave Aggie a brisk hug and kiss too. Holding her big belly, she heaved herself into the seat of the surrey and took the lines Lyle handed her.

"I'll be back; don't you two leave the house."

"Winny?" Lyle asked. He tried to gulp down the question, but it hopped out of his mouth like a frog.

"Are you and the baby okay?"

"I told you this morning," she said. "It's not time."

She met his eyes, so Lyle found himself looking right into her pale blue irises. Her forehead was creased with worry, but she smiled at him. Her smile always turned her face into a heart—the way her cheeks widened and dimpled.

He smiled back.

"Giddup now, Red," she said.

Lyle watched Red jog down Market Street through the drifting smoke. Then he sighed and looked at Aggie. She was drawing in the dirt with the pointed wooden toe of her shoe and didn't look up.

He wondered what to do next. Usually on Sundays between services, the family took turns reading to each other from the Bible, or from the Heidelberger, as Rudy called their catechism book. Then Rudy would play hymns on the piano, and they'd all sing.

He wished Rudy were here. Rudy never got excited about anything (except for trains). Winny always said Rudy and Lyle were opposites, the way Rudy was so big and slow moving, imperturbable, Lyle small and quick and excitable. The only thing that moved fast about Rudy was his hands when he played the piano, and even then, he was so relaxed at the piano bench he made it all seem easy. His eyelids drooped as if he wasn't paying any attention to what he was doing. Then the sound swelled out around him—rich chord changes, runs that went from soft to loud and back to soft again, playful little notes thrown in that made Lyle think of horns or trumpets. At the piano, Rudy played with a dry sense of humor and his face never gave him away. His character came out in the music; you just had to listen.

But he wasn't here to play the piano now.

Rudy and Father were off fighting fire, Winny was by herself looking for lost relatives, and here Lyle was alone with Aggie—Scarlet gone, too—and the world full of smoke. So much was happening, but none of it happening here, now, to him. Or maybe it was happening. Was the fire getting closer? Would his cousins come to stay? Was Winny ready to have her baby? He had no way to know or to stop anything or to take any action. He just had to wait.

THREE

Anders Dirk and Leah Marie

One thing Lyle liked about being around Winny was how she didn't have to talk all the time. And she had this little sarcastic edge that made him laugh. She always managed to say whatever was true, but she wasn't offensive about it.

Just yesterday she had been stirring a pot of hot laundry on the stove, pushing the clothes around with a wooden ladle in the steaming water.

"Rudy says you're too young for Father," Lyle told her.

"I've heard him say that myself. What Rudy means is that I'm too young for him. He'd like an older mother, *dank u zeer*." She said it in that sarcastic way—d*ank u zeer*, thank you very much—only she didn't mean it."

"He says he doesn't want a mother at all."

"He wants his own mother back, and I don't blame him."

"Well, you're not too young for me."

She laughed. "*Dank u,*" she said, and she meant it.

"How come you speak Dutch sometimes?" Lyle asked.

"For the fun of it," she laughed. "*Voor de lol,*" she repeated. "I can hardly live in Holland and not speak Dutch, can I?" She exaggerated her accent. "*Ik ben vijfentwintig.* (I am twenty-five). *Ik ben Amerikaans.* (I am American). I can say *Ja en nee,* (yes and no) *albstublieft en bedankt* (please and thanks), en many *ander* words *dat* are *goede* for me if I want to buy *brood en boter* (bread and butter) in this town. Oops. I mean, *en de stad.*"

Lyle laughed.

She pushed the laundry around with the ladle.

"How come we call people who aren't Dutch 'Americans,' when really, we're all Americans?"

"That's a good question," she answered, forgetting the accent. "Maybe because anyone who's older than twenty came from the old country, and they never stopped thinking of themselves as Dutch, or Frisian, or Zealanders."

"How come you're doing wash on a Saturday?"

"To confuse the neighbors," she said, and he laughed. But when he looked in the pot, he saw it was diapers she was getting ready, and his stomach pulled itself into a knot.

Now he watched Aggie cuddling her stuffed monkey. She patted his back, rubbing the real baby gown as if she were burping him, bouncing him on his diaper.

"You don't know anything," Lyle said. He couldn't help himself.

She frowned.

"Scarlet's over at Mr. Boone's," he went on. "Graafschap is burning, Winny is—" but he couldn't finish about Winny. He just started twirling some lace around in his hand. It was the lace Winny was making. She added a little bit more every night by winding strings in a certain pattern on a tiny loom made from a wooden spool and nails. There were several feet of it by now—enough to go around the bottom of a baptism dress but not enough for a blanket.

Aggie stared at him, her eyes as smoky grey as all the air outside.

"And all you can do is make a stupid cigar joke you've been telling for two weeks straight." He put the loom down on the window sill, letting it make a crisp bang.

"To make you laugh," she said.

"Make me laugh? But why? Great, the city is about to burn down, and you're trying to make me laugh."

"Well, the fire didn't come yet," she said. "You're a big worrywart fraidy cat. I have to cheer you up."

"Oh." Lyle said. "Well." He couldn't think what to say next. "You're a silly billy…" he hesitated. "You're a silly-billy bravie-cat. Here." He pulled her closer so he could fix some of the white-blond hair straggling out of her braid.

Lyle's hair wasn't white like Aggie's. His was brown and cut in a circle around his head like a bowl. Aggie and Lyle both had almond-shaped eyes, but Lyle's were green instead of blue. Father said Lyle got his green eyes from Uncle Bernard, and Lyle liked that because Uncle Bernard had a great beard, too. It was thick, black, and curly, rolling off his chin in waves. Lyle was hoping for one just like it—whenever he was old enough, that is. Or just a little before.

Aggie let him fix a few strands, then brushed his hand away.

"I know something you don't," she went on.

"About what?"

"About Winny, and that's all I'm going to say." She suddenly became absorbed in changing Monkey's diaper and wouldn't look up. "About Winny and her baby," she added.

"What about her?"

"Say you're sorry." She angled her face as she concentrated. "Ouch!" she said, jerking when she poked herself with the pin.

"What about her?" Lyle repeated.

"That hurt," Aggie said. "I'm bleeding."

"Tell me!" Lyle said.

She sucked her finger, then searched for more blood. "Say you're sorry."

"I'm not the one who poked you."

"Say you're sorry about saying I don't know anything."

"I'm sorry. Now what about Winny?"

Aggie got the diaper pinned this time—one excruciating moment at a time.

"Honest—I'm sorry. I'm sorry, really. I'm lucky I have you for a sister. Tell me and I'll—"

"Anders Dirk," Aggie said.

"And I'll never be mean again." Lyle paused. "What did you say?"

"Anders Dirk."

"Who's that?" Lyle asked.

"Or Leah Marie."

"What about them? Who are they?"

"The baby's name. Anders Dirk if it's a boy and Leah Marie for a girl." She smiled at him.

"Really? Winny told you that?"

"Anders Dirk after Grandpa." Then she began burping Monkey, and Lyle looked out the window again at the livery. A team of horses trotted out of the driveway, and Mr. Boone shut the barn door behind them. But Lyle couldn't see Scarlet.

"I don't like babies," he said, feeling that weight in his stomach again as he remembered he used to beg his mother for another little sister or brother.

"I love babies," Aggie said to him.

"It's bad luck to name a baby before it's born," he added.

"Winnie doesn't believe in bad luck and neither do I."

Lyle didn't answer. He just leaned into the window pane. It was easy for her. She didn't remember the funeral. He moved Winny's basket of lace into his lap so he could sit in the window seat.

He stroked a piece of it between his fingers, trying to discern from the looks of it if the baby would be a boy or a girl. Leah or Anders. But he couldn't tell a thing.

Finally Red trotted back into their driveway pulling the surrey.

"Come on," Lyle yelled to Aggie as he let the door slam behind him. He opened it again to stick his head back in the house and added, "Sietze and Jenny are with her and so's Rudy."

He ran to Winny, so she dropped the reins and put a hand on each of his shoulders to step down in front of him, the way she did with his father. Only, his father would have taken her by the waist and landed her gently on the ground. A waft of smoky air blew up from her skirts as she turned to help Jenny down. Rudy lifted Sietze down on the other side.

Jenny and Sietze were three and four years old. They both had wide, fat cheeks that stretched even wider when they smiled. They weren't smiling now, but their eyes were bright with importance.

"*Hallo*," Lyle said.

"*Hallo*," they answered, and Sietze told him, "The fire horses ran past our house."

"And Father rang the church bell," Jenny added.

"Really? Did you see the fire?" Lyle shuddered as he unharnessed Red.

"It ripped through a street of houses," Rudy said, his face grim. "It's still on the edge of town, though, *God dank*."

"Where's Aunt Reka?" Lyle asked Rudy, as Rudy unbuckled the crupper from around Red's tail. "And where's Father?"

"She stayed," he answered. "She's trying to save some things from the house and wanted to know the kids were safe."

"A whole street of houses gone?" Lyle felt that sick feeling in his stomach again.

"Their house isn't in danger—"

"yet," Winny cut in, "but I brought the kids back anyway. They saved the church, and they saved the school." Then she added, "so far."

Red had foam running down in dirty streaks from where the harness turned her sweat to lather.

"I didn't work her that hard; it's just hot," Winny explained as Lyle began rubbing the sweat dry with burlap.

"Do you think the fire will come to Holland?" Lyle asked.

"I don't think so. No one seems to think so," Winny said. "They say the fire won't come. In Graafschap, it's under control; look, the wind has calmed down."

Lyle realized it was true about the wind, but the smoke was worse than ever.

Winny put her hand to her forehead. "Still," she added, "Mr. Post is on his roof watering his whole house down. He's got a ladder, and his children are pumping water at the well and sending buckets up to him."

Rudy walked by Mr. Post's house every week on his way to Hope Preparatory School to take piano lessons. Sometimes Lyle walked along. Mr. Post was another American like Winny.

"Will that keep his house from burning?" Aggie asked. "We could water down our house."

"They say the fire won't come. In Graafschap, it's under control."

She was right about the heat. It was the warmest October Lyle remembered. Summer had seemed to go on and on, right into the fall, and the trees and the ground and the gardens had gotten as dry as the tinder Winny used to start the fire in the cook stove. He shuddered. Then he followed the little kids toward the house.

Winny stopped to lean against the door frame behind him, pressing her hand on her belly again.

"Does it hurt?" Lyle asked her as she straightened up to go inside. "Are you okay? Do you want me to get the midwife?"

"No. The baby's just pushing, that's all."

"Pushing to get out?" Lyle asked.

"No, just pushing." Then she snapped, "I don't know; I never had a baby before," so Lyle bit his tongue to keep from asking any more questions.

Leah Marie or Anders Dirk, he thought. The baby that could take Winny away from him.

FOUR

The Underground Organ

The first time Lyle woke up that night was when the midwife came in, complaining about the wind.

"They always pick the worst weather to be born in," he heard her say. Her voice floated up the stairs sounding placid and soothing, just the way she looked, so Lyle had an image of her broad quiet face. She would be taking Winny's hand and making things seem like they could only turn out okay. He stiffened himself on the sheets, holding his head just above the pillow, craning his ears to hear more.

"How far apart are they?" Mrs. Cox asked, and Lyle heard Winny mumble a response. He poked Rudy in the back.

"Wake up. Winny is having her baby," he whispered. "Mrs. Cox is here."

"I know; I heard."

"How do you suppose Winny got a hold of her? Father's not even home."

"I don't know; maybe Widow Reis went for her. Put the sheet back over your head; you're letting in all the smoke. Just go to sleep."

"I can't," Lyle said. But the talk downstairs was too gentle, and straining to hear every sound somehow did put him back to sleep, because the next thing he knew, he heard his father slam through the door, heard the wind catch the door and whip it against the house.

"The fire broke!" he shouted. "Get the children." Then he must have seen Mrs. Cox because he added, "God help us; why now of all times?"

Lyle and Rudy sprang out of bed even before Father came running up the stairs.

"Oh, good," he said when he saw them. "Put on as many layers of clothes as you can. Right over top of your nightshirts. Aggie! Sietze! Jenny!" he called. He pulled open the curtain where all three were sleeping in the bed beside the fireplace.

Lyle stumbled to his chair where he'd thrown his Sunday outfit, his chest pounding from getting up so fast, and booming from the dark and the smoke and the sound of a fierce wind whining against the house. He put his church clothes on clumsily, not bothering with buttons any more than he could help. Then he pulled his everyday pants over his good ones and buttoned the flap up.

Aggie couldn't seem to wake up so suddenly, so Rudy tumbled her out of bed and helped her step into a petticoat and skirt, then pulled a dress overtop even as she blinked limply into the smoke.

"It's like a hurricane out there," Father said to them all, and Lyle could see him trembling as he pulled a blouse over Jenny's head. "We thought we had it under control and then the wind, my word. I thought we could save everything, and the next thing I knew, the wind came, and I wasn't even sure I could come warn you in time—my own family." Father wrapped the blanket from Aggie's bed around her shoulders.

Jenny broke into loud wailing.

"It's too warm," Aggie protested over Jenny's cries, but her face was somber, and she began helping Father gather the blanket over her shoulders. In the candlelight, her chin looked stiff and strong, so Lyle knew she was trying not to cry.

"Shhh," Father said to Jenny, but he didn't seem to expect her to hush.

She just kept on crying, "I want my mama."

"Rudy, help get Sietze dressed. *Nee.* Never mind, just carry him downstairs," Father said.

Sietze hadn't awakened when Lyle shook him, so they tucked his clothes on top of him as Rudy picked him up in both arms.

"That's enough," Father said as if he were picturing the fire—picturing it getting closer. "Down the stairs, hurry."

Downstairs, Winny was still lying on her side in the closet bed next to the big fireplace, the curtain pulled open. Lyle hoped wildly that she had had the baby already, but he could see at once that her belly was still huge. She looked up at him, looking as wide-eyed as he felt, but he didn't know if it was the fire or the baby coming that gave her that look.

"Just you lie still till the last minute," Mrs. Cox told Winny. Then Mrs. Cox greeted the children, more as if they were entering a church than running from the fire. "Shhh, now, sweetheart," she said to the wailing Jenny, bending down to her and brushing her hair away from her sticky, puffy cheeks. Jenny did shush, amazingly.

"You'll need to stay calm," she told them. "Rudy, that's right, you just carry the little one. Lyle, you hold hands with the other two and don't let go." She put Aggie's hand into Lyle's hand on one side and Jenny's on the other. "It's beyond windy out there," she added, and Lyle had the feeling she thought one of the little children would blow away if he didn't hang on tightly enough. He moved his hand up from Jenny's tiny sparrow hand to her wrist instead. Father was gone and Lyle realized he must be hitching Red to the surrey. Then he blew back into the house in a plume of smoke to lift Winny out of the bed. Mrs. Cox opened the door and the three of them disappeared into the wind again.

"Monkey," Aggie cried out suddenly. "I just about forgot Monkey," and she dropped Lyle's hand to run back up the stairs.

Lyle attached Jenny's hand to Rudy's elbow then followed Aggie. "Hurry," he told her, but he slipped into the bedroom to see if there was something at the last minute that he could bring. He stuffed a ball of string into his pocket—tied full of trinkets and jacks—and then stopped at the wash basin stand in the hallway. Father's watch was open on a towel, so he flipped its silver doors shut then dropped it into his other pocket.

"They're ready," Rudy yelled, and Lyle lunged down the stairs to the door, holding it against the wind just long enough for Aggie and Jenny to catch up, and then he held both of their wrists as they burst out into the hurricane. The wind blew so hard he had to steady himself against it and help pull the girls along. He realized the wind earlier in the day that had snapped the flag so crisply had only been a stiff breeze, the kind you could breathe in and run with. But this wind was different. You had to bend into it to walk. It made people stoop over. It made horses and oxen turn their rumps to it, still hitched to carts.

Though he couldn't see any fire, the world was strangely lit. He could vaguely see the angled rooflines of every house up and down the street. He coughed against the smoke, and the wind sucked the noise of the cough away.

At the surrey, Winny was already in the front seat, sitting up, with Mrs. Cox beside her stroking her arm. Rudy lifted little Sietze up to Mrs. Cox.

"Where's Mr. Boone?" Lyle shouted to Father, looking at the closed-up livery.

"Get in the back," Father shouted. "Here, we better have Jenny up here," he added and pulled her up into the front seat, too.

"But Scarlet!" Lyle answered.

"The horses are rented out," his father shouted back. "The barn is empty."

Father had tied Cookie to the back of the surrey, her tail tucked tightly against her rump, her eyes fringed in white. She was trembling.

He lifted Aggie into the backwards back seat of the surrey. The canvas top strained taut against the wind, as taut as a drum and roaring like one too. Together Rudy and Lyle hopped up on either end of the seat.

"Easy, Cookie," Lyle murmured, though he couldn't hear his own words.

"You ... out ... be ... hang ... on to—," Father demanded. "We can't ...you . wind .. so we ... you ... tight." Half the words blew away in the wind, but they understood well enough to hang on.

Then Father climbed into the front seat, bulky and oddly shaped with his layers of clothes.

Though the air was dense with smoke, and though it was the middle of the night with too much smoke for a moon to shine through, an orange light came down from the sky. Then Red trotted out of the driveway, lifting her head in a long, shrill whinny.

When Lyle heard the answering whinny from the Boone stable, he wasn't even aware of making any decision, he just found himself on his knees in the dirt driveway where he landed, and then he heard Rudy land behind him.

"Scarlet's still in the barn," he shouted into Rudy's ear.

"I know. I heard her, too."

Then Lyle heard a high gasp as Aggie landed on her hands and knees on Market Street.

"Oh great," Rudy said.

Aggie was on her feet and running toward them, bent into the wind.

"I want to come with you," she shouted. "Don't go without me."

Lyle caught her by the wrist again. "Come on. We'll just get Scarlet, then catch up and follow behind the surrey." They ran for the stable.

Together they slid open the big squeaking livery door, fighting to keep the wind from catching it. Scarlet nickered again. Then another horse nickered, and another. The barn was half full.

"We've got to bring them all," Lyle gasped, but for the first instant, he didn't know how they would manage it. He stood in the barn door, staring.

"Aggie, you find Scarlet," Rudy said in his steady way. "Take her out to the hitching post—you're going to ride her. Lyle, we'll just bring them out, one at a time. We can each ride one and lead the others—as many as we can. Aggie will be all right on Scarlet."

Lyle felt suddenly confident again. He knew what to do.

He opened the first stall door and saw Jack, his harness already on. He glanced up and down the dark barn, and to his surprise, he saw the gleam of the silver buckles on the restless horses. They were all harnessed and waiting. But no one was there to take them except him and Rudy and Aggie.

Jack nickered and Lyle trotted him through the door and out to the hitching post, trying to keep him quiet despite the wind. Aggie had found Scarlet, so Lyle tied both horses to the hitching post, his hands fumbling frantically with the ropes.

"Don't get stepped on," he warned Aggie. "Here, quick," he said, and Lyle gave Aggie a leg up onto Scarlet's back, right over the harness. He put her hands on the polished silver hames of the collar, then reminded her to curl her toes to keep her shoes from falling off since there were no stirrups. He wouldn't want her to lose her shoes.

Now she would be safe from the horses' heavy hooves as the nervous animals swung back and forth at the hitching post.

Rudy led Queenie out, then disappeared again. Lyle ran into the stable, found the fourth stall empty, and urged Tulip out of the fifth stall. Rudy passed him on his way in for one more horse and called, "this is the last one." Rudy didn't know their names.

"Satin," Lyle called to him, squinting through the smoke and recognizing Satin's ghostly white blaze standing out in the dark. "That's Satin."

Within minutes, Lyle and Rudy had hitched the four livery horses and Scarlet to the hitching post.

"We need something to use as reins," Rudy said, and he went looking in the Boone barn. The long reins, or lines, of the harness were looped over the horses' collars, and were too long and heavy to use for riding.

The wind blew so fiercely the horses shifted back and forth at the hitching post, their manes flying.

Every few minutes Lyle could see a cart and oxen drift by, or someone would go by half running, half walking. Occasionally someone yelled something through the orange haze—"come on," or "hurry"—but the wind caught the words out of their mouths, so they seemed far away. Lyle's eyes stung, and he couldn't always squint hard enough through the smoke to see who it was out on the street. He concentrated on getting ready.

Lyle and Rudy did hurry, running in and out of the strange barn with the strange stalls they had lived next door to, but never seen the inside of. Lyle kept talking to the familiar horses whom he had never petted. "There you go, Jackeroo," he said, snapping on the lead rope, or "Easy, Queenie." Rudy had found lead ropes to use as reins.

Lyle gave Rudy a leg up onto Jack, and led Tulip up along his right side, so Rudy could lead her with his right hand. Then he fixed the rope reins for Aggie. When he saw Monkey in Aggie's hand, Lyle quickly tucked him into the harness for her. The monkey hung from his armpits, looking around. "Hang on to the reins with one hand," he told Aggie, "and hang on to the hames with the other. Don't let go."

"I won't," she said, and Lyle could see she was scared, and that she wouldn't let go.

Lyle climbed onto the hitching post and vaulted from there onto Satin's back, right over the harness like Rudy and Aggie had done. He untied Queenie himself, leaning sideways over Satin's neck.

"Good girls," he said to both, their ears turned toward him. "I'm ready," he called into the wind. "Where are we going?"

Rudy didn't answer for a moment, and Lyle realized that neither of them knew. And they had taken too long by now to catch up, anyway.

"We'll just follow everyone else," Rudy shouted. Then he turned Jack away from the barn. Aggie followed Rudy, and Lyle followed Aggie with his two horses.

Lyle was glad Rudy set the pace at a slow jog trot. With Queenie beside him, pushing into him, or pulling at her rope, it was hard to go any quicker.

In the light from the street lamps and the ominous orange glow, Lyle could see other people walking or jogging in the same direction. He would have thought they were all heading for a picnic, or a parade, if it wasn't for the strange things they carried along, and it hadn't been the middle of the night. One of his neighbors carried an open basket that turned out to be full of china dishes. Another woman was carrying an oval framed picture that she tried to keep turned away from the wind.

They passed a man digging a hole, and the hole was so deep, nothing showed of the man but his head. The shovelfuls of dirt sprayed up over the edge, making the horses roll their eyes and snort at it, stepping sideways.

"He's going to bury that organ," Rudy shouted back toward Lyle. A small pump organ lay on its side on the dry grass, with blowing leaves whipping against and then over it.

The hole was almost big enough already. Lyle imagined the organ in the hole, and how the dirt landing on the white keys might make the organ play as it landed. The organ would make a sad, eerie tune, he thought.

He shivered and kept a tight hold of Satin's reins. He was glad Mr. Boone had dependable horses. He always liked the idea of prettier horses, hotter horses, horses with some fire. But even old reliable horses had fire in a fire, and it was all he could do to keep a tight hold of the ropes. Beside him, Queenie, when Lyle tugged the rope to slow her down, tended to cut him off by circling ahead of Satin, or she'd push them sideways. Her eyes were wide with the white edge showing how nervous she was.

Lyle saw a chicken coop with an open door, and a girl chasing the chickens out. The chickens were pale orange in the strange light. She clapped and chased them, so the chickens went squawking out into the yard, stretching their necks forward and pushing their legs out behind them. The girl ran past the house, and the chickens, who never stopped running, made a circle back into the coop.

Then a sudden roar filled the air, so the horses tucked their tails, and the children ducked their heads. Something boomed. A shot of pain hit Lyle's ear drums. When Lyle looked back, he could see the glow of flames through all the smoke. Sparks were spraying straight up into the sky like fireworks and then raining back to earth again.

"It's the tannery," a woman shouted over the ringing in his ears. "If the tannery goes, the city goes." The woman carried a basket and held a little girl by the hand, but now she dropped the basket, hoisted the girl up piggyback, and began to run.

Lyle remembered the huge pile of hemlock bark and wood chips outside the tannery. The pile was as high as the roof. The bark was for tanning leather, and the chips were for running the new steam engine. Those chips would never run the steam engine now

FIVE

The Tannery Goes

I'm scared," Aggie cried as Lyle trotted up beside her. Her face was white, and her eyes were red, so he felt a jolt of panic himself.

"You're doing great," he shouted. "You're hanging on great." Behind them, the tannery was a mass of flames so high and so wide it seemed the whole world was on fire. The horses had been trotting out fast, and finally they cantered.

They had to canter past a man pushing a wheelbarrow, so Lyle held Satin back and fell in behind Aggie again. A sewing machine lay in the wheelbarrow.

Soon it wasn't just leaves blowing by, but leaves and ashes, or leaves and sparks, or even leaves and hot cinders. When one of the cinders landed against a horse, the horse would bolt sideways, his rump tucked under. The horses cantered faster and faster. Aggie bounced along on Scarlet, and when the light was right, Lyle could see Monkey's arms flying up and down.

Then, in front of them, suddenly a road burst into flames. It was the newly re-done road, smooth, up-to-date, and made of the circular slices of logs. Within moments the flames made a wall.

The horses piled up around each other, snorting and blowing, their flanks heaving. They couldn't go across.

"The lake," Rudy shouted to them, and then took off the other way. They couldn't be far from Black Lake. If it hadn't been for all the smoke, they would have been able to see it between the houses.

Behind them now, Lyle could see where some wooden sidewalks had started on fire, too. The fire whipped out sideways in a surprisingly straight line.

The horses were already cantering, snorting, prancing, when something spooked them, and they all turned in a bunch and bolted across the street. Lyle held on as best he could, but felt a rope pull out of his hands. He looked to see if Aggie was still on, and she was, her weight pulled backwards against the speed, but her hands clenched on the hames.

Queenie bolted ahead, her tail straight up over her back and her eyes rolling toward an old man dragging a feather mattress along over his head. The wind blew so hard it pushed the old man and the mattress along, as if he couldn't stop even if he wanted to. Then a spark lit into the mattress, and about the same instant Rudy shouted for the man to drop it, the mattress burst into flames. The man's eyes sought Rudy's, but his thank you got blown away. Queenie bolted even farther ahead, then turned.

The roaring of fire, and the wind blowing, and the leaves scuttling and trees bending made the air so thick with noise and ashes that it seemed no new sounds could penetrate it. Lyle saw Queenie raise her head and open her mouth in a call, her head and throat trembling with the strength of it, but he couldn't hear her whinny.

Then they all bolted together toward the orange water, lunging and splashing into it in a frightened bunch. Queenie's rope danced and jerked along the water, but Queenie, in relief at having Satin near, turned her head over Satin's neck, so Lyle caught the wet rope again.

The lights of boats dotted the lake. Some of them had lanterns in the bow, their lights bobbing in the short, rough waves. The kids turned the horses along the shore and trotted and splashed along the edge of the lake. The smell of the splashing water made it suddenly easier to breathe, but still the wind blew so hard, it sucked the air right back out of Lyle's nostrils. The fire roared.

The sky glowed bright through the hazy smoke, as if the sky itself were on fire. He remembered the chickens he'd seen run back into the chicken coop.

The horses jogged along in the water, more controlled now, stepping and splashing over logs or working through bunches of cattails. The play of light on the water and the wind whipping the surface made it hard to be sure of the footing, so the horses kept stumbling. Lyle could feel the mucky bottom sucking at Satin's feet beneath him.

Lyle thought they would be out of danger if they could stay in the water, but suddenly Rudy yelled, "Stay back!"

For a moment Lyle thought Jack had fallen with Rudy, but then he saw him lunging and straining up against the sucking ground. He had mired. He lunged back toward them onto firmer ground.

"God almighty," Rudy said. He turned back toward them, and the horses huddled again, quickly turning their rumps into the wind. "We can't go any farther that way."

"Now what?" Lyle called.

"Can we go farther out into the water?" Rudy shouted. "Wait out there while the fire goes by?"

Lyle tried to imagine being in the water as the fire burned past. Would the water heat up? How far out did they need to be to keep from being boiled like rabbits in a stew? It would be crazy, he thought, to drown just when they thought they were safe from the fire. "I don't know," he said.

Rudy coughed.

"Remember how we pick huckleberries every summer?" Aggie shouted.

"*Ja?*" he asked.

"Well, there's that path. That path made of logs."

Rudy brightened, and Lyle breathed a deep breath, too, thinking of the corduroy trail that the Ottawas had made through the swamp.

"*Ja*," Rudy said. "It's on this side of the train trestle. If we go along the edge of the swamp—without going in—we should find it."

Black River emptied into Black Lake—the lake that Holland had been built on, and Black Lake connected to Lake Michigan with small streams and then sand dunes. Between Holland and Black River, however, were acres and acres of marshland. Surely, on the other side of all that water, they would be safe. If only they could find the trail, that was.

They waded the horses out of Black Lake and followed Rudy along the edge of the swamp, back toward the roaring fire. Now they had nowhere to run without bogging down.

Scarlet was the one to turn into the path.

"I see it!" Aggie shouted.

Lyle followed behind Scarlet, thankful for her swishing flaxen, glow-in-the-dark tail. On either side the bushes grew right through the muck, but the path itself was slightly higher, made of logs wedged together and sand filled in between them. The horses' hooves didn't sink into it.

"Good job; just keep going," Lyle shouted up to Aggie.

"I can hardly see," she called back.

Lyle realized it was true; it was getting darker in the swamp, and for once darkness meant safety. Surely the fire wouldn't cross the marsh. Even after the long dry spell, the marsh, at least, was wet.

"It's okay, Aggie," Rudy assured her. "Just let her have her head and she'll stay on the trail." The trail was barely wide enough for two horses side by side, but Satin and Queenie crowded together, squeezing Lyle's leg between them. They were able to see the edges—or feel them—and they didn't step off.

Finally, Lyle saw a ribbon of light ahead, and then Satin's feet found the bank down to Black River. She plunged in behind Scarlet. The horses huddled against each other in the mild current, breathing each other's breath for comfort, or rubbing their faces against each other's necks. The water caught and reflected the light from the sky. The horses breathed in and out in gasps, their wet flanks heaving, the current swirling between their legs.

The smoky church seemed a long time ago already, and so did Aggie's joke about the dominie smoking. Now he saw how her hair blew across her face and stuck where her tears streamed down.

It made Lyle feel like crying too, the way the fire roared behind them and how Aggie held onto the hames of the harness so fiercely. But instead, he looked at Monkey, still watching from under a leather strap, and agreed with Rudy when Rudy suggested they climb the other bank, out of the river, where they would be safe.

SIX

The Baby

"She's getting closer," Aggie said, looking toward the orange-lighted lake. "What do you think she's carrying?" Aggie had stopped crying now.

The horses stood tied to trees, their harnesses draped over bushes and their bellies still slowly dripping river water. Rudy, Lyle, and Aggie crept along the shore of Black Lake squinting into the smoke at a shadowy figure slowly drifting in a dangerously low-riding rowboat. She had something cradled in her arms and seemed to be trying to rock the boat toward shore in the wind. The current from Black River worked against her, turning the boat one way, while the wind pushed and turned her the other. Her hands weren't on the oars.

"Is it a bundle of something?" Lyle said.

"There's a rope on the bow," Rudy pointed out. "You can see it go down into the water."

"She only has one oar," Aggie announced. "What if that's a baby? It could be a baby wrapped in a blanket."

"It is a baby," Rudy said. "I'm sure of it."

"We better pull her in," Lyle said.

"How?" Rudy asked. "None of us can swim that good."

"Horses can swim," Lyle said.

Lyle and Rudy looked at each other. Yes, horses could swim, but could they swim and pull a rowboat? Could they swim with a rider on their back and pull a half sunken rowboat at the same time? In the dark?

"Poor little baby," Aggie said.

The rowboat made another turn as they watched, but it didn't get any closer.

"Satin's the strongest," Lyle said. "I could swim her out there." Already he felt affectionate toward her. She had gotten him here safely.

"I should be the one to go," Rudy said. "Since I'm oldest."

"No, I should go," Lyle said, "since I'm lightest. How do you expect a horse to swim with you on its back?" It was true. Rudy weighed at least fifty pounds more than Lyle.

"Hurry," Aggie said. "That poor little baby's out in that boat and now she's going to drown! And the old grandma too."

Rudy said, "Let's get Satin ready."

Lyle caught Aggie's hand and followed Rudy back to the shadowy horses. The orange light hung over the lake, like it had done over the river, but under the trees the darkness was so thick it had weight. Lyle untied Satin and slipped the bridle over her head again, more by feel than sight.

"We'll put the harness back on," Rudy told Lyle, "and then you'll have something to pull with."

Lyle took off both pairs of his pants, then stood once again in his nightshirt and shorts.

"Hang onto the hames once she's swimming," Rudy said, "and when you get the rope, twist it around them." As he talked, he gave Lyle a leg up onto Satin's back. "Don't try to pull the boat yourself," Rudy added. "It could pull you right off—just pull the rope from the water and get the loose end wrapped around the hames before anything."

"All right," Lyle said, pulling off his socks.

Lyle guided Satin through the noisy dry fall ferns and down into the water. Satin waded out haltingly, turning her head to call back to the other horses. Lyle stroked her neck.

"Easy there," he crooned. He understood how she felt. The water looked orange and cold, the flames bright on the other side of the lake, making a dull roar. But he kept Satin headed straight into the lake toward the rowboat. The water got deeper.

When the frigid water hit his toes, he curled his legs up as high on Satin's sides as he could, but soon his legs were wet anyway. In a sudden odd surge, Satin pushed off the bottom of the lake, and when she couldn't reach it again, she was swimming. Then she turned back to shore.

The cold water flowing over Lyle's waist and the sudden slipperiness came as such a surprise he didn't even realize she'd turned around until it was too late, and she plunged toward the bank. Or, he thought to himself, he hadn't wanted to go out into deep water any more than she did. He shivered.

"Pull her around," Rudy shouted.

"I am," Lyle called back. He turned Satin around again, facing the boat, and let her stand a minute—knee deep—so they could both be more ready this time. The water and the swimming must have surprised her too.

The woman in the rowboat had seen them now. She yelled and waved. Lyle waved back. Her voice across the water made the lake seem less threatening, so he took a long breath. Now he had a goal.

He urged Satin into the deep water again, more determined. She plunged out, the water splashing. This time it felt warmer on Lyle's already wet legs—better than the wind anyway. Again, she surged forward in the water; again, it flowed over Lyle's waist. He clung to Satin's slippery sides. At first, he slipped backwards with the surging of her swimming, but he grabbed the collar to pull himself further forward. This time he held on even tighter, lying over her neck and gripping the reins hard, pulling her straight, first one way, then the other, as she tried to turn back to shore. She swam with her head held high, just over the water, her mane sweeping behind her in waves.

"You're a good girl," he told her, keeping his eye on the boat and feeling the black water wash through his clothes. He had never been swimming at night before, much less on a horse. It was eerie.

As they got near, Lyle saw at once how low the old woman was in the water. The inside of her boat was half full of glowing water. Her shoes were floating like little boats themselves. He tried to get a look at the baby, but the woman pulled the shawl around her arms to protect it from splashing. Lyle concentrated on the rope hanging down and guided Satin closer.

Grabbing the rope was easier than Lyle expected it to be. He was level with the ring on the front of the boat and Satin wanted to go back to shore anyway, so he just let her turn. All he had to do was drop the reins and catch the slippery rope. He let the rope slide through his hands like Rudy had said. Then, pulling the slack up out of the dark water as fast as he could, he twisted it in a double figure eight over the hames. He tried to give the boat a pull with his own hands, but it didn't budge.

A moment later the rope snapped tight. Satin dropped lower in the water, and the rope, stretching straight back from the hames, slowly pushed Lyle off her back as it crossed over her rump.

His hands never left Satin's collar, but his head dunked under the water before he could help himself and he came back up sputtering. His nightshirt felt clingy and heavy. He clung to Satin's collar, his chin above her neck and her mane floating against his collar bone. For a moment Satin's head was barely above the water. All he could see of her was the white of one wide eye and her blaze parallel with the water. He could feel her lunging attempt at swimming low under the water.

"Kick your feet," the old woman called, in Dutch.

He kicked his feet.

"*Goede!*" she shouted. "Kick them hard and hold tight."

He did kick hard and then Satin's swimming raised her higher again, moving along. The rope from the boat crossed Satin's rump again, steadying itself straight down her spine as she aimed herself toward the other horses on shore. The boat came tugging along behind.

Lyle kicked and splashed, feeling lighter now, steadying himself with the collar. His heart beat hard, and he wondered what would happen if Satin stopped pulling, and they sank right there in the lake? He was thankful for her swimming so steadily, her neck all black and glistening from the water, straining forward.

Eventually Satin's feet found bottom. Her back suddenly rose above the water, and Lyle's feet hit bottom too. He hopped lightly along beside Satin, keeping his bare feet away from her big steel-shod ones. Water ran off and through his nightshirt.

The boat's bottom scraped right up onto the dirt and ferns before Rudy helped stop Satin. Satin's flanks heaved in and out.

Lyle stroked her, and then rubbed her forehead while Rudy and Aggie untangled the rope from the boat. Lyle used his hand to slick some of the water off her gleaming blue-black coat. He leaned his face on her neck, meaning just to rest himself for a second, but he found himself gasping and sobbing into her mane. Lucky he was already wet anyway, with puffy eyes and his hair dripping down, so no one would know how scared he'd been, and how thankful for Satin pulling so hard through the water.

The water drained slowly from the bottom of the boat and the old woman continued to sit there, pulling her black shawl farther over her shoulders. Her shoes were in one bony hand now, her shawl draped over the bundle in her arm. She had turned her grey, striped petticoat up over her skirt, and both were turned over her lap to keep them dry, but her long black stockings were soaked. Her feet disappeared into the muddy water slowly draining from boat.

"Can I see?" Aggie asked.

"See what?" the woman asked.

Aggie gestured to the bundle. Her face lit up and her eyes turned tender.

"Why, sure," the woman said proudly. "Can you imagine I kept it dry all that way?" She pulled the shawl back and then unwrapped a couple of tea towels.

They stared, and Lyle realized for the first time what she carried in her arms—a big round loaf of bread, with the bread knife still stabbed through it. She smiled and held it away from her shawl for them to see.

"Bread?" Lyle said. He couldn't hold back a gulp of laughter.

Aggie's face turned serious in her confusion, and then despite the fire, despite everything, she began to giggle. Then Rudy joined in, and his voice cracked, and that made them all laugh even harder. The woman looked at them sternly from one to the other.

"What's so funny?" she demanded.

"We thought it was a baby," Lyle said, swiping at his eyes with the back of his fists. "We thought you had a little baby in your arms."

The woman's face crinkled into smiles. "Ha-ha. You thought my bread was a baby?" She rocked it, laughing and trembling. "Sweet little bread loaf," she crooned. "You thought you were saving a baby, and here it is just an old woman and a loaf of bread. Saved first from fire, and now water."

"You saved that loaf of bread from home?" Lyle pulled his wet shirt around him. Laughing made him feel better, despite shivering.

"Right off my kitchen table. Oh my," she said, her voice changing keys. "Aren't we a sight?" She poured the water out of her shoes and gestured all around with them. She included Lyle with his wet nightshirt and hair, the steaming, dripping Satin, her own wet stockings and her skirt turned up, even all their puffy eyes swollen from the smoke. In the background, across the lake, the fire glowed.

"You sure could kick," she added approvingly to Lyle.

"*Ja*," Aggie added. "You should have seen all the splashing."

Lyle did feel proud of his kicking, remembering how Satin could swim again once he helped her. He patted her neck again.

"Are you okay?" he asked the old woman. He felt rude not knowing her name. The truth was, she looked familiar. With her eyes swollen and her knees showing, though, he couldn't think who she was. She seemed a hundred years old.

"*Ja*, I'm okay, sure," she said. "I don't know if I can get out of this boat, though. My knees are all locked up. Can you help me?"

Together Aggie and Rudy took the woman's arms, steadying her as she creaked her way out of the boat. Her back didn't seem to want to straighten out. Lyle didn't move any closer. He shivered in his wet nightshirt, too pushed flat by the wind to move.

"Son, you're wet; you'll catch your death." She looked around at the other children, piercingly, as if they might produce a towel out of their pockets. Then she thought of her own shawl.

"Here," she unwound it with one hand, carefully shifting the bread from hand to hand. "You take off those wet things, then wrap this around you. It's good and warm; I made it myself."

"I have dry clothes," he said. "Two pair of dry pants and one shirt."

"Good," she said, and he saw she expected him to change right then and there.

When he hesitated, she gestured to her own knobby knees in their black stockings. "When there's fire and water," she said, "it's no time to get bashful."

He moved away into the blackness and pulled off his wet nightshirt. He started to use the shawl as a towel, until he wondered if it wouldn't be better to leave it dry, if they might need it as a blanket. But in the wind, he was almost dry. Rudy brought him his clothes, so he pulled on his old trousers and shirt again, folding the Sunday ones and putting them in the ferns. He laid his wet nightshirt over a tree branch where it might dry. All the while, the old woman kept on talking, her voice sounding more and more familiar.

Lyle tried rubbing his feet clean with some dried-up ferns, then pulled on his socks. His wooden shoes felt smooth and familiar, so as he pushed his feet into them, he suddenly remembered.

"Mrs. Flikkema?" he asked.

"Why, that's right," she said. She looked carefully at each of them. "And you must be the Hemmis children. I'd recognize your father's ears anywhere."

Mrs. Flikkema lived on River Street. She was so old she rarely came out of the house. She didn't even go to church anymore, that's how old she was. Lyle remembered going to her house one time when he was little, and she had given him peppermints. And now, here she was, rescued out of a rowboat and stranded in the woods with them, without even a place to sit down.

"Which one of you plays piano?" she asked, looking from Lyle to Rudy.

Everyone seemed to know about Rudy's piano playing. Lyle gestured that way.

"I'd like to hear you play once," she said.

Then it hit them: Rudy's piano. Surely it had gone up in flames by now.

"We'll get you a new piano," Lyle said. "I'm sure we will. Even better than you had before. A grand piano." Lyle knew he was exaggerating, but suddenly Rudy without a piano seemed like himself without horses, or Aggie without Monkey. He realized that they had saved the horse he loved, and Monkey was dangling in Aggie's hands right this minute, but he didn't know where a new piano would come from. Or where they would put it.

"Oh dear, oh dear," Mrs. Flikkema said. "Everything we mention is likely burned. Lucky we've got our skin. Where are your folks?" she asked.

"Oh," Lyle groaned.

"We don't know," Rudy said. "We got separated."

"And worst of all," Lyle said, "Winny was having her baby."

"No," Mrs. Flikkema said, her jaw dropping in denial. "Not tonight."

Lyle groaned again, nodding his head. "Mrs. Cox was with us. But we lost them. We jumped out of the back of the surrey."

"Oh. Well then," Mrs. Flikkema said, recovering her brisk tone. "If Mrs. Cox was with her, she'll be all right. What do you mean, you jumped? Why did you jump?"

"We jumped out to save the horses," he said. "We heard Scarlet whinny from Mr. Boone's barn, and we all jumped out. And here Winny was in the front seat about to have her baby!"

"You can't have her baby for her, now, can you?" Mrs. Flikkema said. "But if you saved the horses—and it looks like you did—well, then, that's the important thing."

"We've got to find them," Lyle said.

"You will," she said. "But not this night, that's for sure." They looked around again, squinting into the wind to look across the lake at the raging, orange light. "Whatever's left of it," she added.

"How come you only had one oar?" Aggie finally asked.

"Oh, I had two oars. It's my own fault. I reached out with it for my hat, see. My hat blew off my head and landed in the water. I took the oar out of the socket, trying to reach that darn hat, but I should have known better."

"And then you dropped the oar?" Rudy asked.

"It was heavy," she said. "My bread was about to fall out of my lap, so I dropped the oar and saved the bread."

"Maybe you could have gotten the first oar with the second one," Lyle said. "Did you try?"

"No. I told myself, make do with one, that's what. One's better than none. I can just imagine what my son Harmen will say about losing that oar. He thought he ought to stay right with me to begin with; I told him I could get along."

"Where is he?" Rudy asked.

"Oh, wherever he's got to by now in a boat of his own. He and Jenny and the children. I don't know. We'll find them, I'm sure. We were going to try to stay together, but on a night like this—" she lifted her hands to show what chaos it all was. "Wind, waves, big boats with lights, little boats without lights. *Dank God* for the fire so we could see at all." Then she realized what she'd just said—thank God for the fire. "You do have to thank God even for trials, you know," she added. "Harm was worried about putting me in a boat by myself, and I told him, I came two thousand miles across the Atlantic Ocean in a ship—The Scandia. I'm sure I'm not worried about little Black Lake in a rowboat."

"Were you scared?" Aggie asked.

"Oh, you bet I was. I was sick. Seasick for three days."

"In the rowboat, I mean?" Aggie asked again. "In the dark."

"I was scared I was going to get the bread wet, that's what," she said. "Imagine keeping it dry all that way." She looked at the loaf admiringly. "Harmen, you know what he brought with him?

First, he gets his pipe and tobacco. Then he takes the trunk from the living room and puts it in his boat. You know what's in the trunk? Books, that's what. I ask him, what good's that going to do? You can't eat books. You can't pull them up to your chin at night to keep warm now, can you?"

She looked sharply at the children as though they might disagree.

"Now, me, what I brought was bread. Fresh yesterday, and not a slice gone. I took the blankets right off my bed, and the loaf of bread right off the table."

They looked into the boat and, sure enough, now that the water had run out, they could see the wet blankets under the seat.

"We could hang them on a tree branch," Lyle suggested. "That might dry them out."

"I'd say we could build a fire," Mrs. Flikkema said, "but we've had enough of fires for a while, don't you think?"

SEVEN

The Sound That's Left After Singing

Lyle couldn't remember ever being so tired. He shivered only partly because he had been wet. The night was dry and warm. But he felt exhausted and scared and responsible all at once. It was enough to make anyone shiver. He put his hand up to his chin to keep his jaw from rattling.

The orange glow roared on and on and on.

Rudy lumbered along moving even more slowly than usual as he gathered dry ferns for a bed, and Mrs. Flikkema stood hunched with her shawl over her shoulders near the boat where she'd finally set her loaf of bread on the seat. Lyle dumped an armload of ferns into the pile, then went back for more. Scarlet nickered to him each time he passed, and Lyle patted her velvet red shoulder, feeling guilt stricken. He had nothing to feed her. Ferns weren't actual horse food, though he let Scarlet and the others snatch some on the way by, anyway. In the morning they would have to find grazing.

But the pile was finally big enough and Lyle felt only too glad to sink down into it beside Aggie and Rudy. Then Mrs. Flikkema leaned a hand on Lyle's shoulder, bent stiffly to her knees, turned her backside into the pile and plopped down between him and Aggie. Her skirt and petticoat flew up and then wafted back down.

They all kicked off their wooden shoes and lined them up neatly around their bed.

"What would I do without you children," Mrs. Flikkema said.

"You'd have your bread to yourself," Rudy answered, but they were too tired to even laugh.

"Now let's just all get close together and we can share this shawl for a blanket," she said. "Which side shall we lie on?"

Aggie wanted the right, so they curled up like spoons against each other, Aggie on one side of Mrs. Flikkema, Lyle on the other, and Rudy in front of Aggie. Then they stretched the shawl as far as it would go over them. Lyle thought that normally it would have felt strange to lie so close to a stranger, but somehow in the dark, and after pulling her through the water in a rowboat, Mrs. Flikkema didn't feel like a stranger.

"The wind has died down," Mrs. Flikkema said. "Listen."

Sure enough, Lyle heard the horses stirring in the trees where they were tied, and farther away, the low sweep of the fire. He heard a horse's stomach growl.

"The horses are hungry," Lyle said.

"They'll be okay," Mrs. Flikkema said.

"They're used to having hay," he added. And of all times, they deserved it tonight.

"Aren't you hungry?" she asked.

"I don't think so," Lyle said, trying to think whether he really was.

"Well, if you can get by, so can they."

"In the morning we can find grass for them," Lyle said.

"That's right," she said.

"How late do you think it is?" Rudy asked. "Or how early?"

Lyle couldn't get his bearings with the sky partially lit, but already the night seemed endless. "I don't know," he finally said. "I wonder where Winny and Father are. Do you think they were going to Uncle Egbert's?"

"Maybe," Rudy answered. "If the fire didn't spread that far, anyway."

"I wonder how long before they realized we weren't with them."

"We have to find them," Rudy said.

"I know," Lyle answered. He knew it in the very pit of his stomach.

"They couldn't get to this side of the swamp with the surrey, you know," Rudy said. "They had to run in front of the fire."

"They had a good start," Mrs. Flikkema said. "They'll be ahead of the fire. The wind has died down now. It's burning, sure, but not racing."

"They're probably at Grandma and Grandpa's," Aggie added. "Maybe we can all go live there. Monkey and Mrs. Flikkema too."

He wondered if Mrs. Flikkema's son was somewhere missing her as badly as he missed Winny. "Where do you think Harmen is?" Lyle finally asked her.

"Oh, he's probably got his head on one of his books somewhere, wishing he'd brought a pillow instead," she said. Lyle couldn't tell if she missed him or not.

"I wish we had brought our pillows," Aggie said. Then she added, "I know; I'll use Monkey for a pillow."

"Lucky Monkey," Rudy said.

"I left my blanket in the surrey," Aggie went on. "Remember? I had a blanket wrapped around me, but I didn't want it then."

In the dark their voices trailed on, seeming to float on air, disconnected from their bodies. What they said didn't need to make complete sense somehow. Or it just seemed that way because Lyle was so tired. Rudy stretched and Lyle yawned.

"Do you know what I saw tonight?" Aggie asked Mrs. Flikkema.

"*Nee*," Mrs. Flikkema replied. "What did you see?"

"Two unusual things," she answered. "First, I saw a little boy pushing a toy wheelbarrow, and the wind flew him right into the air. He never let go of the handles before he landed on the ground again."

"Extraordinary," Mrs. Flikkema says. "If I hadn't felt that wind, I might have wondered if you made that up."

"I didn't make it up. I saw it on River Street."

"And what was the second unusual thing?"

"An organ. An underground organ."

Mrs. Flikkema paused. Lyle could hear her trying to form a question, but Rudy helped her out by explaining,

"Somebody was burying it. In the ground."

"Imagine that," Mrs. Flikkema finally said.

Lyle couldn't hold back his own fantasy about it.

"Think of what it must sound like playing underground," he said, and maybe because it was so late on such an odd day, nobody thought that was a strange thing to say.

"What do you suppose it's playing?" Aggie asked.

Then Mrs. Flikkema began to hum. Her voice was low and trembly against the ferns and seemed small in the night air, barely bigger than the sound of the fire, even though the fire was so much farther away.

"We Gather Together," Rudy said, recognizing the tune.

Mrs. Flikkema went right on humming. Rudy began to hum too. Lyle and Aggie listened, and it didn't seem very different from listening to Rudy play piano before going to bed. He had a nice voice, even when he was only humming, and even when it was gravelly from too much smoke.

Finally, Rudy and Mrs. Flikkema quit humming, and Aggie's breathing went heavy. The ferns prickled Lyle's skin and he only had a corner of the shawl, so he gave in and let himself lean into Mrs. Flikkema's warm back. She didn't seem to mind. He felt Aggie's falling-to-sleep twitches. He lay there enjoying the warmth and his own involuntary twitches and after-shivers. Then he fell asleep listening to the sound that's left after singing.

EIGHT

Mare's Milk

Lyle would have slept a lot longer if it hadn't been for the horses. As soon as the day grew light—even a smoky, hazy light—the five horses became restless, pawing, circling on their ropes, nickering hungry morning nickers.

Lyle sat up with a start in the pile of ferns that had shrunk during the night. Scarlet nickered to him at once, nickering right at him, glad to see him awake.

"Good morning," Lyle called softly to her. All the horses were looking now, their eyes bright. "Good morning," he called to them all.

Lyle's face felt puffy and dry—especially his eyes and nose—and he was cold. He'd been having nightmares so the images of flaming sidewalks and flaming surreys seemed burned behind his eyes. It made him especially glad to be awake. Instantly, he began making plans about how to feed the horses.

The shawl had made its way over to Aggie in the night. Rudy rubbed his eyes, and then Aggie jerked her arm.

"Winny?" she cried, and Lyle could tell she was still asleep. She didn't remember where they were.

"Shush, now. It's all right," Mrs. Flikkema said.

If it hadn't been for the horses, Lyle would have felt as lost as Aggie seemed to be, but the pawing, stamping horses dominated everything else. They needed grazing. They needed water first, and then grazing, and Lyle himself would have to hunt for it.

There were ferns—dried ones—close to the shore of Black Lake. But the trees of the forest were so tall that the forest floor itself was clean and dark and rich smelling—with nothing on it for the horses to eat.

Lyle knew that the lumberjacks had logged most of the forest on the north side of the lake. Sometimes on a crisp winter day he could hear the loud crack as a tree went down. There had been a lumber camp over there too. The lumberjacks sometimes came into Holland to buy supplies.

"Let's ride the horses along the lake until we find a place that's been cut over," he said to the others. "There should be grass there."

"Why, *goede morgon*," Mrs. Flikkema said.

Lyle knew he should have started out more politely, but he couldn't stop his head from twirling with plans.

"Good morning, Mrs. Flikkema," he answered, and then he went right on. "I could pull you in the rowboat on Satin again. You know, this time just along the shore. Satin can wade and you can ride in the boat. That way we can get them someplace to graze. They're hungry."

"*Ja*, and I bet you are too," Mrs. Flikkema said. Her eyes were swollen, too, and her thin grey braids had come unpinned from the back of her head, so that they fell down her shoulders in wisps. In the daylight for the first time, Lyle saw how frail she looked, with her red skirt and grey striped petticoat.

"Can you give me a hand up?" she asked him.

Lyle jumped to his feet and took both her hands, but she was so stiff, they didn't make any progress.

When she still couldn't get up, Rudy started pushing her up from behind.

"That's the way," she said. "Just put your shoulder into it and we'll get these old bones off the ground."

Then she was on her feet, Lyle left looking at Rudy's freckles and the twitching corners of his mouth.

"Have you ever heard of arthritis?" Mrs. Flikkema asked. "Arthur, he was the worst of those Ritis boys."

The brother's eyes met, and they burst out laughing. Mrs. Flikkema's joke was the invitation they needed to get the laughter out.

"Get it?" Aggie asked. "Arthur ITIS." She laughed happily. Lyle could tell it wouldn't be the last time he'd hear the arthritis joke from her.

When Mrs. Flikkema retrieved her loaf of bread from the seat of the boat, she held it against her shoulder to cut into it, spoke a blessing, then gave them each a thick slice.

The bread tasted so good—so thick and grainy—that Lyle had to slow himself down, chewing deliberately slowly. He knew there would only be one piece. There was still lunch and dinner to get through. But the piece was big, and he was satisfied.

"You're glad I brought bread and no baby," Mrs. Flikkema said.

"We're going to have our own new baby pretty soon," Aggie offered. "At our house." Now that she was awake, she seemed content again. She had the clear imprint of a fern along her cheek.

Maybe, Lyle thought, maybe we'll have a baby, and we'll still have Winny when it's over with, but it wasn't something you just assumed. Live births were miracles.

"That's what I heard," Mrs. Flikkema said. Her face turned grim for a moment and Lyle knew what she must be thinking: how horrible to have a baby now of all times. But she saw Lyle looking at her and her face brightened. "What a blessing," she said. "Babies are always blessings."

"We don't have a house anymore," is all Rudy said.

"I know," Aggie answered, and finished her bread.

Scarlet's udder was hard and tight with milk. Lyle wouldn't have noticed if it hadn't been for a thin sharp white stream making a track across his shoe as he stepped around her. He ducked his head under her belly to look. Her udder was so hard it glistened. Then he caught the stream of milk in his mouth. It felt sharp on his tongue and tasted nutty. Sweet and nutty. When it stopped, he stroked the velvety, glistening skin, then gently squeezed the teat. The milk zinged across his nose and into his mouth again.

He stood up for a second to see where Rudy and Aggie were. "Hey, everyone," he called. "Anybody thirsty?" He gave himself a couple thinner squirts of milk and then stood back to see what Scarlet thought of it all. She had tucked up her flank, as if holding her breath, but that was it. She did the same thing when Cookie nursed from her.

Aggie picked her way toward him across the velvety, hummocky ground, her skirt and petticoat hiked up so that her bird-like ankles showed. "What do you mean?" she asked.

"Milk," Lyle called. "Come get some milk."

"I'll have some," Aggie said. "I'm dying of thirst."

Aggie crouched under Scarlet's flank, so Lyle aimed the teat toward her and hit her in the eye with the stream.

"Hey," she said. She wiped away the milk with her sleeve but didn't back away.

"Open your mouth wider," he instructed her. This time the milk streamed in.

"Look, the other side's dripping too." She pointed to the milk volunteering from the other teat, then ducked all the way under Scarlet's belly and came up on the other side. "I'll take this side; you can have that one."

They kept the milk flowing until Scarlet's udder went slack and the streams of milk got thin and short.

"I bet that feels better." Lyle straightened up.

"It was delicious," Aggie said. "I sure do."

"I meant Scarlet." Lyle ran his fingers through her flaxen tail. "Scarlet feels better."

Rudy had his hands stuffed into his pockets and stood watching them from the shore. "How'd it taste?" he asked.

"Delicious," Aggie said.

"Good," Lyle said.

Rudy swept his arm out toward a pretend audience as if making a grand introduction. "Welcome to my family," he said, then he cupped his hand around his mouth and added, "We're not related."

Lyle and Aggie laughed even as Aggie protested, "But it was excellent."

"I bet," Rudy said. "But I'll stick with water."

"Lake water?" Lyle asked.

"Good point," Rudy said. "We can drink out of the lake if we get thirsty enough, I think." He said it tentatively. They called Black Lake "black" for a reason.

Lyle petted and looked over each horse, stroking his hands along them. He found an angry burn the size of a silver dollar on Queenie's rump and understood why she jerked the rope out of his hands last night. Tulip and Jack had a couple of freckle-sized burns, but otherwise the horses were unscathed. He would need ointment for Queenie's burn, but since nothing came to mind, he focused on getting the horses to grazing.

Aggie and Mrs. Flikkema folded the blankets they had spread over a couple of bushes to dry. Lyle and Rudy harnessed the horses with the parts they needed and placed the rest of the harnesses into the rowboat. After the horses drank long and deep from the lake, they waded along the shore, the boys each with their pair of horses and Aggie by herself on Scarlet, heading the same way around the lake as they'd been going the night before. The difference was that Satin pulled the rowboat behind her as she splashed along, and Queenie, beside Lyle on a lead-line, didn't dance in excitement. She placidly pulled against the rope for wisps of weeds that grew along the edge of the water.

Mrs. Flikkema sat in the rowboat, once again cradling the remains of her bread loaf wrapped in tea towels and a shawl, looking for all the world like a bundled-up baby again.

Compared to the night before, Lyle thought, the world seemed comfortingly quiet. All he could hear was their own splashing. No one said anything, even when one after the other they got splattered by swishing horse tails that whisked the grey water out of the lake in a sloppy spray. In the morning chill he was thankful for the warmth of Satin's back. Everything seemed grey—tinny grey water, tinny grey smoke, tinny grey sky, all reflecting each other so that Lyle thought if he bit down hard, even his mouth would taste like tin.

There were still boats on the water with their anchors out, but even more boats were pulled up along the north side of the lake. Black Lake was smooth, without a ripple to show there had been waves the night before. The town of Holland itself was still a mass of dark smoke, with shoots of flame here and there. Lyle preferred not to look in that direction. Instead, he peered into the woods, trying to find a glade of grass.

The rowboat tugged along behind him, lighter this morning because it hadn't leaked itself half full of water yet. Nobody said a thing until they came to a tree that had fallen into the water and blocked their way. Lyle thought for a moment that Satin and he would have to swim again to get around it, but Mrs. Flikkema suggested they portage instead. So, Rudy tied his horses up, then helped Mrs. Flikkema out of the boat. Lyle simply rode Satin slowly up on shore, around the high tipped-up roots of the tree, dragging the boat noisily behind him. Rudy helped guide it, and then Satin was back in the water, and Mrs. Flikkema back in the boat.

They had barely gone any distance when Lyle saw what he'd been looking for—some cut trees. Then suddenly they were in a clearing of wide tree stumps, and the horses nickered when they saw the almost-green grass.

The children rode the horses right into the midst of the glade, then gave way to their pulling to let them plunge their noses into the feast.

"You found a clearing," Mrs. Flikkema commented approvingly. "It's an old half-cleared slashing the shanty boys left behind." She gripped the sides of the rowboat as it bumped onto the shore. "Lumberjacks, they call them these days," she added.

"How come they call them shanty *boys*? They have shoulders like Paul Bunyon," Aggie said, "And I don't call that a boy."

Mrs. Flikkema smiled. "Because they live in lumber camps full of shanties"

"They have beards and chew tobacco, and I don't call that a boy, either." Aggie added. "Dominie VandePol says they're a nest of sinners."

"He pretty much thinks that about everybody," Rudy said.

"How come the shanty boys live in shanties instead of real houses?" Aggie pressed on.

"The shanty boys work for one logging outfit after the other, that's why," Mrs. Flikkema said. "They log what you call round forties. They log forty acres in the middle of a land parcel, then clear the next forty acres on every side like a honeycomb before they move to the next camp."

"Is that why the shanty boys start fires and leave them?" Aggie asked. "Because they're moving on anyway?"

Mrs. Flikkema laughed again. "They're cleaning up," she answered. "Or anyway, that's what they say."

"That's what everyone's always arguing about," Rudy told her as he slid down from Jack and took the bridle off. "They start the fires to clean up the mess from the slashings—all those branches and brush. Otherwise, you can't get through on your own two legs, much less with a team and wagon. At least the fires leave some cleared land … or so they say." Rudy jerked his thumb toward the smoke across the lake. "They're leaving a lot of cleared land all right," he added.

"Cleared land," Mrs. Flikkema repeated. "That's one way to put it. Heaven knows how far the fire has burned."

The question of how far the fire burned took moments to contemplate as they looked at each other. It could have been as far as the next county. It could have been as far as China or the moon, that's how far their raging imaginations went.

"Now what?" Aggie finally asked, opening her hands to show that the horses were eating grass. They had arrived somewhere.

Lyle realized he hadn't thought that far ahead. He was just happy that the horses could eat. Still, it would be nice not to have to hold the horses all day while they grazed.

"Why don't you children make a corral," Mrs. Flikkema said. "Use the tree branches. The shanty boys left you plenty of branches right here anyway."

It was a perfect idea.

"Maybe you could hang on to Satin while she eats," Lyle suggested to Aggie. "The rest of the horses will stay near her. They won't go anywhere once they've found good grass. We'll just let them loose."

Aggie sat on a stump while Satin grazed all around it, and meanwhile, Lyle and Rudy began dragging branches to fill in the gaps from stump to stump. At first, they were ambitious, trying to enclose the entire glade, but finally they realized they'd have to make it smaller—more like the corral outside the livery. Lyle pulled branches from inside the enclosure outward, and ones from outside it inward, pulling and tripping occasionally over other downed junk. Loggers left a mess behind them, he decided, but from the number of rabbits that jumped out from under his feet, he realized that at least the mess made shelter and grazing. Finally, he unbridled Satin so Aggie would be free again, then watched as the horses browsed.

His mouth didn't taste so much like tin, now.

NINE

A Spoon, a Stopped Watch, and a Diaper

Lyle unwound his string full of jacks on the bow of the grounded rowboat for the others to see. Rudy kneeled outside the boat while Aggie crouched just inside it, in the little triangular space of the bow in front of the front seat. Mrs. Flikkema sat on the other seat, where she'd been when they pulled her in, since there didn't seem to be any better place to sit. Her head was bowed. When Lyle had unraveled the last jack, a marble, and nib of a fountain pen from the string, Aggie put her monkey on the bow, then they both looked at Rudy. He dug into his pocket and brought out a spoon. He held it out in front of him, his face looking so puzzled, his forehead wrinkling, that they giggled.

"Why did you bring a spoon?" Lyle asked. Their only worldly possession looked so ridiculous he couldn't help wiping his eyes and laughing.

"I don't know," Rudy said. "It was on our chest of drawers, and I remembered Winny told me not to leave it there. I stuck it in my pocket."

"One monkey, one string, five jacks, a spoon, a marble, and an ink-pen tip," Lyle said.

"A diaper, a baby shirt, and two safety pins," Aggie added, pointing to what Monkey was wearing. "If we count what Mrs. Flikkema brought, then we've got a bread knife, a loaf of bread, and two blankets."

"Two-thirds of a loaf," Rudy corrected. "And she'll need the blankets for herself."

Then Lyle remembered something. He rummaged through his clothes, and finally dug his hand into the pocket of his Sunday trousers. Just what he thought: there was his father's silver pocket watch. Stopped. He held it up to his ear.

"It's Father's watch," he said. "But it's not ticking."

Rudy looked at it with appreciation. "Let me see," he said. "It probably only needs to be wound." The stem whirred and clicked as he turned it. "What time do you think it is?"

Lyle and Aggie looked at each other. "Noon?" they asked.

"Twelve o'clock," Rudy said, as if by announcing it he made it true. He pulled out the stem and turned the hands. "Think how happy Father will be when he sees you saved this."

"*Ja*, and think how happy Winny's going to be about that spoon!" Lyle answered. They laughed some more, so Mrs. Flikkema looked up. Had she been sleeping that way? She wanted to know what was funny.

Aggie showed her the spoon. "Rudy saved it from the fire," she said. "It's just an old soup spoon, not even one of the silver-plated ones."

"My grand rescue," Rudy said. "A spoon."

"What's wrong with that? Now you'll have something to eat with," she said smugly. "Those two will be eating with their fingers, but not you."

"Look, I brought this string." Lyle wanted to hear what she'd say about that.

"Hmm." She looked at it. "It's dirty. What did you use it for in the past?"

"Cat's Cradle, see?" he said, and deftly strung it between his hands. He held it toward Aggie. She hooked her fingers into it daintily, then flicked her wrists and ended up with the string stretched between her hands in a crisscross pattern.

"Well, then keep on as before," Mrs. Flikkema said. "And if you need to tie up a package, then you'll always have it handy."

Lyle set the jacks spinning on the bow of the rowboat, trying to see how many he could spin at the same time before they wobbled to a stop or collided with each other. He had four out of five spinning when Mrs. Flikkema suddenly stared over his head. "Look," she said.

Lyle heard splashing, and when he craned his neck, he saw a man drawing a rowboat along the shore toward them in long strokes. His back was to them, but he kept turning to get his bearings.

"Maybe that's my Harmen," Mrs. Flikkema said. "He'll be looking for me. He thinks I'm lost."

"You're not lost," Aggie protested.

"But he doesn't know that. Oh dear, I hope it is him. He's probably hungry."

The man in the boat did not turn out to be Harmen Flikkema. It was Harold Bos, the man who took the portraits. His long, bent nose and twisty black eyebrows looked darker than usual, and the circles under his eyes were black. He looked even more serious now rowing his boat than he always looked carrying his important black camera in its big black box or ducking under the camera's black hood to take someone's portrait.

Mr. Bos recognized Mrs. Flikkema first. "Good morning, *Mevrouw* Flikkema," he said. "How are you? Is everybody okay here?"

"*Goede morgen*," Mrs. Flikkema answered. "Oh, we're doing all right, sure."

"*God Dank*," Mr. Bos said. He drew his boat up behind theirs and looked intently at Rudy.

"It's the Hemmis children," he announced. "Where are your folks?" He looked around as if they might be coming out from the woods any minute now.

"They're not here," Rudy said. "We lost each other."

"Lost them?" he asked.

"We got separated," Lyle clarified. "We're going to find them as soon as we can." He said it louder than he needed to.

"Oh, sure they're all right," Mr. Bos said. "*The Lord is our only comfort in life and in death.* Don't you worry." Then his voice went low, and he gestured toward the smoky remains of Holland. "I just came from over there," he said. By the look on his face Lyle could tell it wasn't good news, but that he wanted to tell it, that he even relished telling it. "What's left is still burning. If it doesn't rain, there won't be one building standing."

"Nothing at all?" Mrs. Flikkema asked.

"I couldn't get in far," he answered, "smoldering the way it is. Smoldering in some places, flaming in others, so I can't promise that nothing is left. But I can promise not much is left. Everything is sheared off to ground level—every house, every tree. And anyone who didn't get out...." His voice trailed off. "At least we've got those who fled to this side." He looked at Lyle again, sympathetically, then at Aggie, who still had her hands held out in front of her, looking at the network of string as if it were some fancy drawbridge she was crossing in her imagination.

"Those who fled to the other side, I don't know how they would have survived." He shook his head sadly. "You two sitting here playing Cat's Cradle and spinning jacks. You should be praying. Thanking God for being alive. Well," he added briskly, "the Lord giveth and the Lord taketh away," and he dug his oars into the water.

Aggie crumpled her hands and let the string go into a wad, then passed it cheerlessly to Lyle.

When the man was gone, Lyle gave his string a fierce tug, so it broke at the knot. Playing Cat's

Cradle when there was a tragedy, he thought. Smoke still billowing across the lake, Winny and Father lost somewhere, and them acting just like kids.

But Mrs. Flikkema frowned after Mr. Bos. "He should be thankful you are sprite and well-fed," she said. "I'd rather see children playing than crying, any day. I was going to offer him a piece of bread," she added, "until I saw he was going to be nothing but doom and gloom."

The kids slipped their treasures—the jacks, the spoon, the watch—out of sight again and sat quietly now. The smoke hanging over Holland weighed Lyle down.

"How are we going to find them if we can't get through town?" Lyle finally asked. He didn't have to say who he meant by "them."

"We've got to wait till the fire is burned out," Rudy answered.

"If only it would rain," Mrs. Flikkema said.

In church, Dominie VandePol had been praying for rain all summer. Lyle spread his elbows out on the nose of the boat so he could lay his head in his arms. Out of the corner of his eye he could see the horses scrounging and picking through the weeds in their glade, so he turned to face them, then closed his hot eyes.

"Remember when Mother died?" Rudy asked Lyle, so he opened his eyes again. Now Aggie was slouched over, too. She didn't look up.

"*Ja*," Lyle answered. How could anyone forget?

"That's how this feels. Like a story that's not real. You tell other people about it—that your Mother died—but you don't believe it yourself."

Lyle nodded, watching Rudy's face.

Rudy looked across the lake. "So, I wonder when it's going to hit us."

"It comes to you in small ways," Mrs. Flikkema said. Rudy and Lyle both turned. "Tragedy does, you know. For instance, if you have a child die of the pox, you miss that baby every dinner time. Maybe singing a psalm before dinner, you miss her small voice. Then at supper, you feel there's a portion for her even though she's gone. And saying prayers at bedtime, you still pray for her, but she's not there. Isn't that how it is? For you, losing your mother, too?"

Lyle nodded.

"And comfort comes in the same small ways. You three gobbling up your slices of bread like it was a feast—that's a sight that'll stay with me." She sighed and smiled at them, then bowed her head again, her grey braids still flopping loose.

This time Lyle turned a little so he could lay his face down directly on the boat, warm from the sun. It had been a short night.

He woke up when he heard more splashing. He thought that Mr. Bos had come back, but this time it really was Harmen, rowing a boat and then bounding over the end of it onto dry ground so he could throw his big arms around Mrs. Flikkema. For a moment, Lyle thought he would lift her out of the seat, he was so big. Aggie and Rudy and Lyle all looked up at him and stared. It wasn't what Lyle expected from someone who saved his books from the fire.

"There you are," he said to Mrs. Flikkema. "Harold Bos told me where to find you." He kissed her cheek, so her face seemed to disappear into his blue-grey beard. Harmen wore dark Sunday clothes like Mr. Bos. The only difference was, his collar was loose at the neck, and if he were taking portraits, the people would smile.

Mrs. Flikkema's face finally came out of his beard. "We saved you some bread," she said, unwrapping it. "You'll have to be thankful it's a loaf of bread and not a baby, of course."

"A baby?" he asked.

"We thought her loaf of bread was a baby," Aggie explained. "We thought she and the baby were going to drown, the way the wind blew them around and around."

"Tell him about pulling the rowboat," Rudy said to Lyle. "How Satin swam and pulled the rowboat."

Harmen looked at Lyle, but Lyle felt suddenly too ridiculous to tell the story. It didn't even seem true right this instant in the daylight.

"If only I hadn't lost an oar," sighed Mrs. Flikkema.

"It's a good thing Satin didn't sink," Aggie added.

When the story seemed too mixed up to ever get straight, Harmen asked who Satin was, who went swimming, and what they were talking about. Lyle finally had to point the horses out to him so he would understand about Satin pulling the rowboat.

Harmen whistled. "How many are there?" he asked.

"Five," Lyle said. "Tulip, Satin, Scarlet, Queenie, and Jack."

"You mean to tell me that first you saved those horses from Boone's livery stable, and then you swam one of them out into Black Lake and pulled in Mother in her rowboat?"

"In the dark," Mrs. Flikkema said.

"The fire brings out the best in people," he said. "Do you notice that? Last night we were all heroes, and today we're all refugees."

"Heroes?" Mrs. Flikkema asked.

"I saved my books," he said. "You saved your bread. The children saved you. That reminds me," he added. "Is anyone here thirsty?"

"*Ja*, dying of thirst," Lyle said. Scarlet's milk already seemed like a long time ago.

"I am," Aggie and Rudy both added.

"I found a spring off a creek that feeds into the lake," Harmen said. "I filled this bucket."

"Ha, so you did save something useful," Mrs. Flikkema said, approvingly. She approved and scolded at the same time, Lyle thought.

Harmen's grin pushed his beard back. "It was in the boat already. Here." He held the dipper out to Aggie first. "Drink off the top—there's sand in the bottom. Don't swirl the bucket."

Aggie drank first, then Lyle, and the water tasted good—clear and coppery. It was still cool, and he filled the dipper again and again.

Finally, when everyone had drunk, Mrs. Flikkema cut small pieces of bread for the children and a thick one for Harmen. "What do you hear?" she asked. "Do you have any news?"

"Chicago," Harmen said.

"Chicago?" Mrs. Flikkema's thin grey eyebrows raised.

"Chicago burnt down. And Peshtigo."

"Chicago! No. How can it be?"

"Yes, the Chicago fire is going to go down in history as the greatest tragedy of the nation. But Pestigo was worse. There are horror stories from Pestigo."

"Peshtigo? Where's that?"

"Up north Wisconsin. Bustling boom town. Logging town. It's a wall of flames and not enough survivors to report the death toll."

"Who says that?" Mrs. Flikkema asked sharply.

"The crew from the steamer that runs from Green Bay to Chicago."

Lyle looked at Rudy and Rudy looked at Aggie. Chicago was the biggest city they even knew of, though they had never been there. Lyle had never heard of Peshtigo, either. It seemed like the whole world had burned.

"The crew described whirlwinds of fire along the shores in Wisconsin. Fire tornadoes, fire balloons, fire devils."

"But what started it?" Mrs. Flikkema asked.

Harmon shrugged. "You know what the wind was like yesterday. In Chicago they say it was the O'Leary family's cow, whoever they are. Mrs. O'Leary's cow kicked a lantern over. But logging practices being what they are, what do you expect? The lumber companies leave debris in piles to dry for tinder. They start controlled burns here and there, magically thinking they'll stay controlled. Add enough wind and—"

"Poof," Rudy said.

"Lumber barons get rich, and our hard work goes up in flames. Whole families burned to—" He glanced at Aggie, suddenly hesitating.

Aggie looked up. "Burned to a crisp?" she finished.

"Yeah," he said. "In Peshtigo, whole families burned to a crisp, and other families drowned. Houses with skeletons in the ashes."

"Tell me about Holland," Mrs. Flikkema interrupted, glancing at Aggie. "What about Holland, right here? If it's not too gruesome," she added.

"No one knows of anyone for sure who got hurt in Holland," he went on, "but there are rumors. They say that Mrs. Agema had her baby right out in the middle of a plowed field, but her feather mattress caught fire and they both burned up. But Mr. VanDyke said he saw her, and she's fine—it's a baby boy. Everyone's so scared, they're sure that someone else is killed."

Lyle stared. A woman had a baby in the middle of a field? He thought about Winny and shivered. The story could be true; they'd just mixed up the names.

"They're saying only the ones that fled to this side of the lake could have made it—that the fire would burn all the way from Chicago to Holland, then north to Grand Rapids and take anyone in its path."

Mrs. Flikkema cleared her throat.

Harmen looked at Lyle and then Aggie again. "That's just talk, though. Scared talk. There's probably a camp of people over on the east side saying they're the only ones who could have made it."

"A camp?" Mrs. Flikkema asked.

"I didn't tell you," he said. "If you go down the lake, you'll see where a group has gathered. There's even a big tent. Someone saved it from the fire—brought it back from the War Between the States. People have been coming in all morning. That's where Jenny and the kids are."

"A circus tent?" Aggie's eyes lit up.

"A brown army tent," Harmen answered. "It sleeps, say, eight people. Or a dozen or more if there's been a fire. We could row on down if you want," he said, looking around at them all.

"Is that where Mr. Bos is?" Rudy asked.

Harmen nodded.

"No thanks," he said.

"I'll go," Mrs. Flikkema said. "Anyone else want to?"

Aggie shook her head. Lyle was glad. He didn't want to be left alone. He missed Winny and Father. He couldn't keep down the gnawing feeling that only one thing mattered: finding them. And even though it was impossible to get back through town now with the fire still burning, he didn't want to leave the horses.

Even as Harmen helped Mrs. Flikkema into the rowboat, Lyle watched Scarlet turn in a circle and crumple her legs. Her knees sank deeper and deeper until she landed heavily on the ground with a muffled plop that made dust rise. Jack and Queenie had given up picking at the weeds and grass, too, and stood with one leg resting, their eyes blinking closed.

Tulip was the only horse still in motion. She stood over a bush and wiggled back and forth, back and forth, her top lip stretched out luxuriously and her eyes half closed. The twigs at the top of the bush worked back and forth into her hide. She had found the perfect belly-scratcher and wore the contented grin of a pickpocket.

Lyle smiled at her.

"We'll be back, then, before bedtime," Mrs. Flikkema said. "Now that I've found such warm sleeping companions, I wouldn't give them up."

Lyle waved as Harmen and Mrs. Flikkema rowed away, then he climbed through the barricade of tree branches to scooch down into the warm boy-shaped nest in the crook of Scarlet's neck. She adjusted her muzzle to rest on the grass by his shoes and closed her eyes again.

TEN

The Free Man

Winny knows you have a crush on her, you know," Rudy said. He sauntered along behind Lyle on a deer path along the lake.

Lyle's ears got hot. He turned around to wait.

"I do not," he said.

"I heard her tell Father. She said it was sweet."

"No. You didn't, did you? You're making it up." Lyle couldn't stand to have her thinking it was just a crush, the kind the girls always got on Mr. Van Oss at the schoolhouse.

"I'm just telling you what she said."

"It's not a crush," Lyle insisted. He considered telling Rudy that he actually, truly loved Winny but decided that would only make things worse. "It's better than the way you treat her, anyway," he added, to get Rudy off track. "You always act like you don't have to listen to anything she says."

Rudy pulled at his nose as if he were about to rub off his freckles. "She's not even old enough to be my mother," he said.

"So," Lyle said. Rudy always used that argument, and Lyle didn't see what it had to do with anything.

"So, I don't give her that hard a time. Just sometimes."

"She is old enough to be Aggie's mother," Lyle told him.

"It's not a big deal. I just don't see how you can still miss Mother and then be so crazy about Winny."

"I don't love Winny the same way. I loved Mother like a mother, and I love Winny like Winny."

"It's disloyal," Rudy said.

"How does it help Mother to be mean to Winny? I just like to be by her," Lyle said. "She makes me laugh."

"Come on," Aggie called from in front of them along the lake. "Catch up. I'm hungry."

They would have stayed with the horses, waiting for Mrs. Flikkema, if it hadn't been for the smell of fish. It had kept wafting toward them, right through the woods and among the horses. Not the strong slimy smell of dead fish on a shore, but the warm toasty smell of fish frying.

Lyle also couldn't help wondering if he could find some first-aid treatment, maybe some oil for Queenie's burn.

They followed the smell along the shore, stepping over tree roots that dipped into the water. Occasionally, they met up with faded deer paths that were so powder dry, the dust flew whenever the children crossed one. Lyle looked across the lake where everything was black and billowy with smoke, sickening to see. Then, thinking of Lot and his wife in the Bible, he said,

"Whoever looks back at the fire turns into a pillar of salt."

It was a contest. They marched forward. Lyle looked to the left and the right but not back. Aggie looked left and right, but not back. Rudy stared straight ahead.

That lasted for about five minutes. Then when a faraway whistle blew, they all looked back at the smoke, and then at each other.

"We're all pillars, then," Rudy said.

"Do you think Lot's wife really turned into a pillar—you know, like a church pillar?" Lyle asked. "Or do you think she just turned into a statue of herself looking back?"

"A statue," Aggie said. "A statue with flying hair."

"A pillar," Rudy said. "It said 'pillar.'"

"It said pillar, but did that mean pillar-like statue? Maybe it just meant she herself turned to salt."

"It's a statue with flying hair, a flying skirt, and a curious face," Aggie said, looking perhaps like the statue herself as she twisted back, glancing at the smoke again.

"I'm too thirsty to be thinking about salt," Rudy said.

Aggie hiked up her skirt so she could scramble over another fallen tree.

"Me too," she said. "Will they have something to drink there, at the fish fry? I hope there's desert too."

"We don't even know if they have enough fish for us," he said. "But I'm hoping someone has some ointment for Queenie."

They went along quietly for a while, negotiating the obstacles along the edge of the lake. Then the three of them rounded a curve in the lake, and there they were, suddenly, at a camp where there was a brown army tent, a cooking fire, a log pile of lumber higher than their heads, and groups of people milling about. The smell of cooking fish was strong now, and the sound of voices stronger yet.

Lyle had expected to see familiar faces, but this crew seemed to be from everywhere. He heard several unknown languages. They broke into English with heavy accents, and among them, of course, he heard Dutch as well as Winny's American English. He saw a man with a burned-off sleeve and a woman with the bottom of her skirt burned around one side. The man with the burned sleeve had a bandage on his arm.

Five or six women bent over the fire, huddled together. Lyle smelled pipe tobacco. To his surprise, he saw a man with skin black as night and his little daughter with kinky black braids. The girl turned her eyes to the newcomers and watched them, but the man was busy scaling fish nailed to a board and didn't do more than glance.

Then the women at the fire saw Rudy, Lyle and Aggie. Lyle wasn't prepared for their rushing or their grim faces.

"Oh, these poor children," the first woman said, and suddenly Aggie and Rudy were jostled away on either side, and Lyle found himself being kissed on both cheeks by not just one but several women in a row.

"Oh," the second woman exclaimed. "These innocent children, left as orphans. And this is just the beginning." She began to weep softly, so her voice came out strangled and uneven. "My grandchildren are lost," she said. "Lost like you. May they come into as capable hands as you have."

"We're not lost," Rudy said firmly, in his slow way. "We're fine. We're not orphans."

"*Ja*," Aggie added, "We smelled the fish and we're—"

"Hungry," Lyle finished. The woman dried her eyes on her handkerchief now. He had to quickly dry his own eyes, too, he suddenly felt so sorry for himself.

"And thirsty," Aggie added, clutching her throat dramatically.

The woman turned Lyle's hands over in hers and gasped again. "Oh my," she said. "You're burned."

Lyle looked at his own horse-dirty palms. "That's just a rope burn," he explained, remembering suddenly the moment that Queenie pulled away from him. "That's all. But it hurts!" he added, since suddenly it did hurt. "Do you have any ointment? I need some for a horse too."

"Oh," she said. "*God Dank*. We'll have to think about that one. What are your names, then?"

When Rudy answered, she nodded her head familiarly.

"The Hemmis children," she said. "I'm Mrs. Grootenhuis. Your father cleans my sewing machine every year." She hesitated. "Used to clean it. So where is your father, then? And that American woman—"

"Winny," Lyle said.

"She must have a new baby by now, is that right? I never heard anything about it."

Rudy explained one more time about the horses and getting separated from their parents as Mrs. Grootenhuis led them to the fire, where the fish sizzled and curled on a rickety-looking grate woven out of green switches.

She swung her head at the news of Winny. "Cursed are those who bear children in those days," she quoted. "Have you got a clean handkerchief, any of you?" she added.

"Monkey's diaper is kind of like a handkerchief," Aggie said.

"And it's certainly clean," Rudy said, straight-faced, so Lyle snorted, suddenly remembering Monkey hanging from his armpits in Scarlet's harness.

Mrs. Grootenhuis gestured for it, then held it open while the other woman used forked sticks like clumsy tongs and filled the sagging diaper with pieces of fish. "Sit down on the bank with this," she said, "Then you can share. Don't burn yourselves, now."

Lyle raked a few hot flakes of fish apart, then tossed one of them into his mouth even as he walked. It was steaming hot and moist, mild-flavored, just how he liked it. They found a place to sit on the bank of the lake.

To the left were the group of people with the accents and the colorful speech. To the right was a pile of logs with ends as big around as flour barrels. The ends of the logs had a brand burned on them, like the haunches of beef cows.

Rudy ate his fish clownishly with his spoon while Aggie and Lyle plucked out the bones, then pushed the thick white flakes into their mouths with their fingers.

Behind them, the women stood near the fire but more in a pose of exhaustion than as if they were really watching the fish cook. Lyle realized they didn't have any place to sit down. Not any place comfortable, anyway.

When Mrs. Grootenhuis saw him looking her way, she straightened up again. "You children must be thirsty," she suddenly remembered. From next to the tent, she picked up a tin bucket full of water—the same one they'd already drunk from earlier that day. The dipper clanged against the edge as she hoisted it over to them.

"Here you go," she said. "Harmen Flikkema found a spring. We all just use the same dipper."

Mrs. Grootenhuis stood uncomfortably over them as they passed the dipper from one to the other. She shifted her weight, then sighed. "It's okay for you youngsters to sit on the ground," she said. "Your knees still bend. Oh, well," and she gathered up her skirts to land down beside them anyhow, the dust rising from the dry ground around her.

"We need rain."

"Who caught all the fish?" Rudy asked.

Mrs. Grootenhuis pointed toward some boats on the lake. "They're out there catching fish now," she said. "Good thing for all these fishing boats, *Ja*?"

Lyle saw the black man coming to Mrs. Grootenhuis with some cleaned fish on his board, his little girl holding the side of his pant leg. Lyle tried not to stare.

Lyle had heard about ex-slaves, or freedom-seekers as some people still called them. After the War between the States, they were all free. Or maybe this man had been free to begin with. The funny thing about calling a black person "free" is that people never said white people were free. Only black people.

Lyle thought freedom-seekers had a heroic ring to it. They started their trip to freedom with nothing—not even their own selves. Lyle looked at the man's brown leather shoes because he was too polite to look at his face. He wanted to though.

Aggie didn't have the same problem. She stared so hard she got up and walked to the girl as if pulled by a magnet.

With her curious black eyes, the girl watched Aggie coming toward her. She gripped her father's pant leg tighter.

"My name is Aggie. What's your name?"

"Marcia Jane."

"You wanna know what started the fire?" Aggie didn't wait for an answer but slid her eyes sideways and squealed, "Dominie VandePol smoking cigars!" She delivered it like it was the most hilarious joke in the world.

Marcia Jane giggled.

Aggie giggled.

"What ship do friends sail on?" Marcia Jane asked Aggie, speaking southern.

Aggie pulled a braid up to her mouth and bit it to help her think better. She raised her eyebrows.

Only then did Marcia Jane hoot, "Friendship!"

They laughed into each other's faces again.

"Ever heard of arthritis?" Aggie asked. "Well, Arthur is the worst one of them Ritis boys."

They threw their heads back and laughed and laughed.

Lyle dared look at the man's face now and saw his eyes crinkle at the corners. He met Lyle's gaze and winked. Then he held out his hand.

"I'm Abraham," he said. Lyle took the warm hand.

"Nice to meet you, Mr. Abraham. I'm Lyle." He felt his brightest smile of the day squeeze his cheeks tight because he couldn't resist. That was one good thing that came from the fire. He saw his first free man.

Lyle was glad Mr. Abraham was free.

ELEVEN

Shanty Boys

"Happy-go-lucky, that's what them shanty boys are," the man with the red beard said.

"He runs the brewery," Rudy whispered to Lyle. They were still sitting near the bank where they had eaten fish, and the group of people around them had grown.

The man with the red beard, the man with the burnt sleeve and some others had pulled and pushed two of the smaller logs down from the wood stack—no easy feat—and now the logs made a V shape near the beach for people to sit on. They sat and chatted, relieved to finally be sitting down.

"Happy go lucky? Is that what you call swearing and drinking and fighting with your fists?" Mrs. Grootenhuis answered. "They make fifteen dollars a month for their sweat and blood, and the real money goes back to a bank out east. The shanty boys just do all the work and face the danger."

"Widow-makers, they call some of them trees," someone said and slapped the log he sat on affectionately.

"How do you figure that? Nine out of ten of those men ain't married so there's no widow to leave behind," Red Beard answered.

"Who earns the money, then, if the shanty boys don't earn it?" a young woman asked. She spoke with a lilting accent Lyle couldn't place. Her blond hair and upturned nose made her look Dutch, so Lyle was surprised by her accent. An older man with a similar upturned nose stood just behind her. He wore a yellow rain slicker and moved his eyes from speaker to speaker. As his look shifted from inquiry to boredom, Lyle realized he didn't understand the conversation.

"Lumber barons who own the lumber companies, that's who earns the money," Mrs. Grootenhuis answered. "They make the investment, of course. You gotta give them that. But they're not the ones who work from dawn to dusk and travel from one camp to the next with their axe, at risk of losing life or limb."

"Or both," Rudy said under his breath to Lyle.

"They take the good with the bad," Red Beard said.

"Mostly bad," Rudy whispered again.

"You Swedes," Red Beard broke in, addressing the girl with the accent. "You're used to forest. You send plenty of your men to be shanty boys.

"Yes," the girl said, "My two brothers are lumberjacks in Muskegon. They will meet us in Minnesota as soon as they save up some money."

Yellow Slicker spoke to her in a quick under-the-breath language. Lyle tuned his ears in to pick out a few sideways words that he interpreted to be *brother, October,* and even *axe.*

"Is that your father with you? How do you do?" said Red Beard, nodding to the man with the yellow slicker. "Do you speak English?"

The father himself answered with a shake of his head and a so-so gesture with his hands. "Little bit," he said. "*Lite gran.*"

He's learning," the girl answered. "My name is Anneli, by the way. What is yours?" she asked, looking toward Rudy.

"Mine's Rudy," he said, his freckles suddenly getting more colorful as a blush creeped up his face. "You headed to Minnesota?"

"Yes, my family. My father and I, we are traveling to Minnesota. We were living in the City Hotel for two nights and did laundry. We were planning the rest of the trip, but the hotel burned..." Her brow furrowed, considering her English. Then she amended, "It burned up. Did it burn down or up?"

"Both!" Burned Sleeve answered. "Holland burned down, burned up and burned every which way to Thursday."

For some reason, everyone smiled now, though it wasn't a joking matter.

"You been traveling long?" Burned Sleeve asked.

"Three months," Anneli answered. "My brothers came to America first. They've been here a year. My father and I sailed across in July. We have cousins in Minnesota."

"Swedes head to Minnesota, Finns head up north, Dutchmen come here, freedom-seekers—" he nodded at Abraham "—come up to Detroit, or Canada, usually. Poles come across Lake Eerie and down to Chicago."

Red Beard nodded at another couple sitting at the end of a log, so Lyle understood they were Polish, "But here we are camped out, the lot of us, lucky if the clothes aren't burned right off our back."

"We all in the same boat, if we lucky enough to have us a boat," said Burned Sleeve.

"That pile of logs there, that'd build some boats or a mighty fine house," Red Beard said.

"Sure would, if it was ours," Burned Sleeve said.

Everyone gazed at the log pile, nodding appreciatively.

Lyle couldn't decide if it was terrible or wonderful to see such a pile of massive logs. It was wondrous in its sheer mass.

"What if Michigan runs out of trees," Aggie suddenly asked. She and Marcia Jane were playing Cat's Cradle with the string Lyle had brought. They held still a moment, looking as if their hands were woven together.

"Run out of trees?" Red Beard laughed. "How do you figure we can run out of trees? The trees are like the stars in the sky. You just try to count them and then tell me we're going to run out."

Burned Sleeve scratched at the edge of his bandage. "Stars in the sky are infinite. You got that right. But it's hard to replace a 500-year-old tree. I don't like those round forties. They should leave one forty out of every circle."

"That'd be a waste of effort," Red Beard countered. "Once they got camp built and make roads, the only thing for it is to cut every forty within reach."

"How many round forties you figure there are in Michigan?" Mrs. Grootenhuis asked.

"Round forties, now I guess we could work that out if we did the math."

"Well, if you can count the round forties, you can count the trees too."

"Trees grow back," Red Beard said.

"That could be. If you got time to wait. It does break your heart when the big ones go, though." Mrs. Grootenhuis added, "I wonder if old Grandfather is still standing."

There were trees in Holland so old they had names. Grandfather was the landmark on Third Street, a huge oak with so many arms and branches it looked like the great-great grandfather of all trees everywhere.

There was also a tree named Lightning on Fish Street. You could see the slash where the lightning had struck the top many years ago. Afterwards, its canopy grew lopsided. Lyle's favorite was Moses, so big around that it took all three siblings plus his friend Pieter with their arms out to encircle it.

"Grandfather is gone, burned up and burned down and burned all the way to Thursday," Red Beard answered.

Lyle saw some startled faces.

"Grandfather is a tree," Rudy said, aloud this time, to Anneli. "*Was* a tree."

Her face changed from concern to relief.

Look," she shivered and held up her arm. "I have goose nipples."

"Goose *pimples*," Rudy corrected her. He smiled an unusually broad smile, for him anyway.

Anneli smiled at him, then laughed. "Right, goose pimples. Thank heaven Grandfather is a tree."

"Where are the Ottawas when you need them?" Burned Sleeve asked out of the blue. "The Ottawas usually show up about the time we need rescuing. I wouldn't mind a trader showing up with some supplies about now. I wouldn't mind a medicine man either with a first-aid kit."

"That hurting you?" Mrs. Grootenhuis asked, nodding at his bandaged arm.

"I'll get by," he said. "I don't suppose anybody saved any ointment from the fire? Or honey?"

The question went unanswered, which Lyle took to mean no.

"Ottawa?" asked Anneli. "Are the Ottawas and Dutch friendly with each other?"

"You bet," answered Red Beard.

"We have had a few rocky moments," Mrs. Grootenhuis added. "But we always end up on good terms again. They saved our lives the first winter—over twenty years ago. They taught us how to make snares and showed us what to hunt for. Helped us hunt meat to keep body and soul together."

"They helped us fell the first trees," Red Beard went on. "We come from the land of dikes. Canals we are good at, trees not so much. Waukazoo's clan taught us to fell the trees to build our houses."

The older people among the Dutch nodded.

"The next year we paid them back with a big ignorant mistake." Mrs. Grootenhuis shuddered. "I'm still ashamed. Some of us found tools in the forest among those big maples. There were axes, troughs, and some kind of tools. We had no idea they weren't just abandoned. Mr. Vanderwal and a few others took the troughs to feed their hogs. Everyone gathered up what they wanted rather than leave good tools in the forest.

"Well, in March, along with the first crow, the Ottawas came back. Turns out they make maple sugar every year. Tons of it. That was their equipment they left in place, and when they came back, it was all gone."

"Ooh, embarrassing." Anneli grimaced.

"They could see a few of the troughs in the hog pens. You can just imagine… that's how they thought we paid them back for getting us through that first winter! But it was sheer ignorance."

"Ignorance is the same as sin," Abraham spoke unexpectedly so the other faces turned toward him.

"We all guilty of it since we ain't omniscient like God. But it hurts people just as bad as being evil."

There was a pause for his words to sink in.

Lyle wondered, from the extra bit of silence, if he wasn't the only one seeing a black person for the first time.

"What are you doing in these parts?" Mrs. Grutenhuis finally asked Abraham.

"Anybody seen a dark woman, the spittin' image of this here girl?" Abraham asked the group, looking around. "Marcia-Jane and I, we be searching for her mama, my wife. We'll backtrack all the way back to Mississippi if we have to, where we got separated."

"Sold," Rudy whispered to Lyle. "She probably got sold."

"After the war, some of my people are still living like slaves, and we're gonna help her get up north. Gonna bring her home."

"What's her name?" Aggie asked?

"Her name's gonna be Hallelujah when we find her." Abraham's face lit up.

"Well, I haven't seen anyone the spitting image of Marcia Jane," Mrs.Grutenhuis said, but we'll watch for her."

"Tell her Abraham & Marcia-Jane are searching for her. Tell her to go to Detroit."

Behind them, Lyle heard footsteps near the cooking fire. He looked back to see who it was. Then there was suddenly rustling, and he could feel the vibrations of someone running.

"Look!" Aggie jumped to her feet.

Lyle looked just in time to see someone tip the curling pieces of fish off the grate into their shirt and run off.

"Did you see that? Someone just stole all the fish. Hey!" Aggie shouted.

Rudy looked at Lyle and Lyle looked at Mrs. Grootenhuis.

Lyle asked, "Who was that?"

Aggie leaped over the log and ran in pursuit, but whoever it was had disappeared as fast as they came. "Someone in a blue striped shirt," Aggie reported.

Red Beard and Burned Sleeve didn't look around in time to see, but the Swedish father in the yellow slicker stood up and shouted, "HEY!" and a string of words Lyle didn't understand.

"Look at us, just sitting here," Mrs. Grootenhuis said. "I can't believe my eyes."

Red Beard stepped over the log as if to follow, but Lyle saw at once how tired he was. He realized all the men were tired. They had been fighting the fire the day before and some had been fighting the forest fire days before that. They had been running for their lives all night, and the sudden disappearance of a grate full of fish wasn't the worst problem in the world, especially when there was more fish waiting to be cooked.

"Help yourself!" Rudy shouted toward the empty place in the woods where the person had disappeared. "Our pleasure!" his voice broke in mock generosity.

"I hope it was raw," Aggie said as she came back. "They could have just asked, you know, like we did."

"Right," Mrs. Grootenhuis said. "That's what it's for.

"Whoever it was, they were hungry," Aggie said.

"*Ja*, that's the thing to remember. They were hungry. We'll have even more fish as soon as some boats get back," Mrs. Grootenhuis said. They stared back at the fire and the tent, and finally Mrs. Grootenhuis got herself to her feet—not much easier than when Mrs. Flikkema got up—and went over to the fire to fix the grate. She opened the flap of the tent and Lyle could see her gesturing as she told the story to some people inside.

"Look," Aggie said.

Now a man in a canoe paddled up. He leaped out over the bow, landing exactly where the water ended and leaving a moccasin print in the sand.

"That's my Frank," Mrs. Grootenhuis called from the tent, rushing back to shore.

"Oh, thank heaven, you're here," Mrs. Grootenhuis said. "When you left, we were a safe camp of refugees, but now it's become a den of thieves." And she told the story again.

The adults stood near the fire talking low; Lyle watched over the lake. Finally, Mr. Grootenhuis glanced with interest in Lyle's direction, then came to sit down next to them. He didn't have any trouble crossing his ankles and dropping gracefully to the ground, cross-legged.

"My wife says you've got some horses?" Mr. Grootenhuis asked. "How many?"

"Five. Scarlet is ours, but we've got four of Mr. Boone's. Five total."

The man looked hopeful. His face became suddenly bright with ideas, but Mrs. Grootenhuis cut in.

"It won't do any good," she said. "Not while the fire's still burning."

He frowned.

"You can't get horses through there," she told him. "They've been rescued once already; just leave them be where they're safe."

Then Lyle realized what they were talking about. Mr. Grootenhuis wanted to use the horses to get back into Holland.

"So, you've got them corralled up, down the lake a way?" he asked, gesturing toward Lake Michigan.

Lyle froze.

"The other direction." Rudy hesitated, then pointed in the right direction when Lyle didn't answer.

"You got any saddles?" Mr. Grootenhuis asked.

Lyle held his breath.

Again, Rudy waited, then answered,

"Just harnesses."

"Bridles?" Mr. Grootenhuis asked.

Rudy nodded.

Lyle glanced imploringly at Aggie. She turned her face up to Mr. Grootenhuis. She clearly got the hint it was time to change the subject.

"How come you're wearing Indian shoes?" she asked.

"You noticed my moccasins?"

"They look soft," she said, holding up her own wooden shoe to compare.

"I traded for them," he told her. "At the Old Wing Mission during the market. My wife likes to stock up on wicker baskets, but I see to it to get a pair of moccasins every year."

Another boat scraped up on shore, and this time it was Harmen, Mrs. Flikkema, and a couple children. Lyle waved wildly at them, happy to see someone familiar. Mrs. Flikkema and Harmen gestured for them to come out to the boat.

"You're here!" Mrs. Flikkema exclaimed.

"Have a look at this mess of fish." Harmen gestured to the bottom of the boat where seven or eight nice fish lay, perch and trout and a couple big bass.

"This'll feed some more hungry bellies," Harmen said. "Can you please help?"

Rudy and Anneli lifted the little children out of the boat, while Lyle ran with the fish two at a time, carrying them to where Abraham had gone back to his board and knife for the fish-cleaning operation.

When Lyle arrived with the last fish, Abraham had wrapped a bit of something in leaves and handed it to Lyle.

"Heard you all need salve for your horse's burn," he said. "This here just some fish skin, but lay it over the burn. It'll protect it."

"Thank you," Lyle said, taking the package of precious leaves. "Thank you very much. Good luck finding Hallelujah."

"Thanks, son. That's gonna be the happiest moment of my life."

After that, Lyle crowded into the boat with Rudy, Aggie, Harmen and Mrs. Flikkema. He showed his treasure—the fish skin laid in the leaves. Rudy sheepishly took a scrap of cloth from his pocket and showed that he had written down a town in Minnesota with Anneli's and her father's full names. "That's where they'll be in a few months, he explained.

"I told Marcia-Jane we're going to say a Hallelujah prayer for her every day. Every time we say 'Hallelujah,' we're going to pray she finds her mama."

"Hallelujah," Mrs. Flikkema, Harmen, Rudy and Lyle all said.

TWELVE

The Other Side

The next morning, Lyle awoke to the sound of the horses as they moved restlessly around their enclosure. One of them stomped; another clambered heavily to her feet. Lyle opened his eyes just in time to see the sudden halo of debris fly around Scarlet as she shook the sleep out of her joints. The horses didn't appear alarmed, he decided. Just alert.

It was too early to think why the horses should suddenly be alert. He lay his head back down and put his nose into Aggie's hair when he heard another sound. He stiffened himself and quit breathing again.

There it was—something falling out of the trees. Possibilities shot through his mind: Acorns? Hot ashes? Cinders? Spiders? He shuddered and thought of Dominie VandePol's sermon about spiders. But no, it wasn't spiders.

And then he had it. Rain. It was the pinging of heavy water droplets falling through the trees. Now one hit him on the lip, and he tasted it with his tongue. The first drops plopped heavy and full, making little explosions in the dry forest floor all around him. Then the rain speeded itself up and slimmed itself down, so the drops became thinner, faster, more economical, and Lyle sat up.

"It's raining," he said.

It came down harder.

Rudy sat up beside him, ducked his head, and held his hands out at the same time.

"*God dank, het regend*," Mrs. Flikkema said.

Thank God, it's raining, Lyle thought, translating for himself.

Mrs. Flikkema turned her face up into the rain. She smiled. "It's raining cow tails and bricks!"

Lyle shook Aggie's arm.

"Wake up," he said to her. "Aggie, it's raining. It's going to put out the fire."

"It's raining water," she said, answering Mrs. Flikkema.

"Run for the boat," Mrs. Flikkema said. "You children can turn it over and get under it."

Lyle and Rudy helped Mrs. Flikkema up, then they grabbed the blankets and ran. Together they heaved the boat over. Then, in another burst of effort, they dragged and lifted the bow onto a nearby stump to create more room. Aggie crawled in under one gunwale.

"Come on in," she called. "It's dry."

The rain pelted Lyle in the back, but he just kept his head ducked and shoved the blankets under the boat to Aggie. "Can you get under there?" he asked Mrs. Flikkema, who had caught up. He realized she had said "you children" can get under, as if she herself wasn't planning to.

"It would be worse torture to get myself under the boat than to sit here and get wet. I'll just sit here and make up new expressions for what it is raining. It's raining hope!" She laughed again.

"We can get the boat up a little higher," Rudy said. His eyes squinted against the rain as he looked around. Then he gestured to Lyle at a hunk of tree roots.

"Help me grab that," he said.

Together they wedged the rotted tree roots under the stern and Lyle wiped his gritty, wet hands on his pants.

"Now try," Lyle suggested to Mrs. Flikkema.

Mrs. Flikkema groaned. "My poor old bones," she exclaimed as she heaved her skirts over her arm one more time and lowered herself to her knees.

"Arthur is the worst one of those Ritis boys," Aggie reminded everyone.

Lyle dropped down, too, and scrambled under the boat. "It's dark under here," he said, as his eyes adjusted to the sudden blackness over his head.

The top half of the world was dark except for a narrow chink of light which explained why Mrs. Flikkema had been sinking the other night.

Mrs. Flikkema was still on her hands and knees. In the dull light coming in under the sides of the boat, Lyle could see her veined old hands and the skirt of her dress under her knees on the wet ground, but her face was in darkness.

"There," her voice said. "Now we'll see if the boat does any better keeping out the rain than it did keeping out the lake."

Rudy's shadowy hands gestured upwards. "It's coming in," he said. "But it's not going to get us wet, looks like." Sure enough, the rain water that came in ran along one of the wooden ribs and dripped steadily off the gunwale.

The ground they sat on under the boat was damp, but when Aggie started to brush away the top layer of leaves and debris, they saw that it was dry underneath. They brushed away all the dampness beneath them, then wrapped themselves in Mrs. Flikkema's blankets and turned around to get lined up together.

The blankets were damp too, but not wet, and still warm from the body heat of overnight. They had to sit between each other's legs one after the other, like on a toboggan, to make room. Rudy sat in the back since he was biggest, then Lyle and Aggie, then Mrs. Flikkema in front of Aggie so she could keep her legs stretched out—semi-comfortably—in front of her.

"Achh, rain," Mrs. Flikkema said. "I know a time we didn't welcome rain so much. Oh. That was a bad summer. All that rain, and cold, and sickness. That's when we built the orphanage."

"Holland doesn't have an orphanage, does it?" Lyle wiggled to get comfortable and found the perfect spot to lean against Rudy's leg without pressing him backwards.

"That's the funny thing about it," Mrs. Flikkema said. "You're right. It doesn't. But we did build one once. It was sad, how many orphans there were those first years. You wouldn't think anyone would die of starvation here, now," she said. "But back then, that's what caused a lot of deaths. All we had was corn the first winter. Thank heaven for the Ottawas or not a one would have made it. Those that survived still had to get through that wet summer. Rain, rain, rain. Not like this year. The first summer was wet.

"Most of us arrived in the fall. We still had to cut trees and make houses. You kids, now. You're used to the trees. These huge old trees." She swept her hands out, so that Lyle involuntarily looked up at the bottom of the boat. "But imagine us coming over straight from the old country. Holland is all canals and drained fields. Field after field, with canals in between and a few hedges and windmills. They build houses out of brick over there, you know. We didn't even know how to cut the trees to build the houses."

"How come you didn't get here in the spring?" Lyle asked. "Then you would have had the summer to get ready for winter."

"Well, sure. That's right. Only, you can't cross the sea in the winter, can you? Some of us crossed in the fall, and others came in the spring, but there we were in New York, and we still had a long way to go. Those who came during the winter got work right there in Albany and we traveled all summer.

Crowded canal boats with mules pulling them. Then railroad. Ships down the Great Lakes. That took all summer, that's sure, and here we were in the fall—about to face a hard winter—and no time to prepare.

"The people that died—oh, it was hard. And then when spring came, the rains came with it and all summer we barely had the chance to dry out. Those that didn't die of the cold died of the wet.

"That's when we gathered money to build the orphanage," she told them. "Dominie VanderMeulen persuaded all the women to give up their jewelry. Most of us had some gold jewelry from the old country, you know. He collected it, and the men started building the orphanage, only, the funny thing is, by the time it was finished, nobody wanted to give up their orphans to go live there. We'd taken them all into our homes, and not one went to live in the orphanage after all."

"What did you do with the orphanage, then?" Aggie asked.

"Used it for a town meeting house." She sighed. "If I'd have known it was only going to be a meeting house, I don't know that I would have given up my brooch," she paused, "not that I miss it. No. I can't say I miss it."

Underneath the boat, their voices went quiet as they listened to the heavy rain.

Aggie leaned her head heavily sideways into the crook of Lyle's elbow, turning her face away from the light seeping in under the boat, and Lyle felt, more than saw, that she had closed her eyes again.

Gradually her body went heavy with sleep against him.

Then Rudy, behind him, leaned his head against the inside of the stern, pulling the blanket up for some padding.

"When it comes to horses, I prefer a steady team of oxen myself." Mrs. Flikkema said eventually. It fit with Lyle's thoughts, who was pondering whether the rain would wash away the fish skin he had laid on Queenie's burn.

"Dominie VanderMeulen, he was the first in *de stad* to have horses. Well, ponies, I guess. He had a team of old ponies, and they weren't young when he got them, either. He'd had them a few years already, and he stopped at my house one day and asked if I'd watch his team while they rested. I asked him, I said, 'will they run away?' And he said, 'No, they won't run away, but they might fall down.'" She laughed at the memory.

"Might fall down," Lyle repeated, and smiled too. "Poor old things."

"So, you and horses," Mrs. Flikkema went on. "You're about as bad as Harmen and his books. When did you start loving horses so much?"

Her tone was gruff, but Lyle knew how much she loved Harmen, and he didn't mind being compared to him.

She had undone one of her thin braids now and worked through her thin white hair with her fingers, trying to smooth it out strand by strand. In the dim light, Lyle could feel the movement of her hands in her hair better than he could see it.

"I don't know," he said. "Every night after I feed the horses, I like to climb up on Scarlet's back, right in the stall, you know. I turn backwards and lie down on her rump." His voice trailed off as he thought about sinking his face into the furry, warm, dusty top of Scarlet's rump.

"Didn't your mother mind you staying out there by yourself?"

Lyle watched while Mrs. Flikkema untangled another braid.

"Well, I think the first time I did it was after she died. I don't mind going to bed anymore, but at first, I hated it without her." He could remember exactly how Mother's fingers felt stroking through his hair—cool and soothing.

"Umm," she said. "Didn't your father help?

"*Ja*, but Aggie was worse off than Rudy and me. She cried herself to sleep every night. Father had to take care of her."

Lyle listened to the rain drumming on the boat, the noise amplifying itself and surrounding him. His back was warm from leaning against Rudy and his front warm from Aggie. The cloudy dull light of the rainy day magnified the wet ground just beyond the toes of his shoes. He could see individual rain drops fall and channel themselves into tiny rivulets that formed small pools and sank into the ground. He stared at the hungry ground sucking up the rainwater.

"Lyle?"

"*Ja?*"

"Listen to me," Mrs. Flikkema said, and her fingers paused in her hair. "Once someone you love dies, your world gets bigger. Not smaller. You know what I mean? Your world is bigger because it's got to include the other side in it, now, too." Then her fingers began moving again, twisting her smoothed-out hair into new braids.

"The other side of what?" Lyle asked. When she didn't answer, he said, "How?" His arm was getting tired, so he shifted Aggie's limp head to his other elbow.

"Well, any boy who can imagine an organ playing underground can imagine heaven."

"It seems too far away," he admitted. Hell felt a lot closer, the way the dominie described it so vividly every week. "Mrs. Flikkema?"

"*Ja?*"

"Who died. I mean, of yours?"

"I'm old," she said. "When you're old, lots of people have died. But I wasn't always old. You wouldn't know it, but I only got old quite recently."

"Who died?" Lyle asked again.

"My first baby—my baby girl. She died of the pox when she was only five."

Lyle watched the rain a moment as the death sank in, then answered,

"That's too sad," because it was. Aggie was five now too. He suddenly remembered her as a baby—a big toddling baby or a little tiny girl, whichever you called it. His mother had still been alive. He could see his mother in her white cap—one of those close-fitting, lacy caps that came down to points around her head. She was playing peekaboo with Aggie behind a sheet hanging down from a doorway.

He supposed the sheet was there to dry; it was raining outside. (Is the rain what made him remember?) There his mother was on one side of it, wafting it back and forth and laughing at Aggie, whose face kept crumpling from one fit of laughter right into the next.

"Rudy?" Lyle said softly.

"Um hmm?" Rudy said. Behind him, Lyle could feel Rudy lift his head off the bow.

"Do you remember Mother's face?"

"Sometimes. Just for a second."

"I wish I could; I try, but I hardly ever remember it."

Winny didn't wear one of those caps like his mother had. It was a Dutch thing, and even some Dutch women didn't wear them anymore. In the new Holland, people were changing their ways. He wanted to tell Winny his memory—if she had lived through having the baby.

Even Lyle's knees ached, and his stomach was growling when the wide ribbon of light all around the boat began to gradually brighten. The hard rain had finally slowed down to a drizzle. Then a pair of wooden shoes stepped into sight.

Someone rapped smartly on the top of the boat.

"*Hallo* in there," the voice said.

"*Hallo,*" Mrs. Flikkema answered.

Lyle ducked his head out from under the edge of the boat and looked up.

"Harmen," he cried. He ducked his head back in. "It's Harm," he said to Mrs. Flikkema. Then he collided with Aggie as they both dodged out from under the edge of the boat together.

"Anybody hungry in here?" Harmen asked. "I would guess the fish are really biting."

"Of course, we're hungry," Mrs. Flikkema answered, her voice sounding hollow and echoey. "Help me out of here, will you?"

"Just a minute; you don't have to crawl out," Harmen said. "Stay put and we'll move the roof off your head." He motioned to Lyle and Rudy to take a spot on the edge of the boat, and they neatly lifted it from over top of where Mrs. Flikkema was still sitting. They set the boat down on the ground this time.

"*Dank u,*" she said. She rolled to her back and reached a hand up for help. Harmen lifted her to her feet without even pretending to let her do it herself.

"There," he said. "Let's go fishing."

THIRTEEN

Hoof Prints

"We're almost to Lake Michigan," Aggie said, twirling the untied sash of her dress as Harmen rowed back along the shore. The drizzle had let up, and even the damp inside of Harmen's rowboat had gone from wet brown to dry grey.

They had been able to look through the channel out through the sand dunes and into the big lake—that expanse of blue-grey that Lyle always marveled at because it was as open and big and deep as the sky.

Rudy wrapped the fish lines around the sticks and poked the fishhooks into the wood so nobody would get caught.

"You can just lay those poles under the seat for the next time we need them," Mrs. Flikkema told him.

They had a mess of fish in the bottom of the boat, and Lyle wanted very much to get them into his belly.

"Listen," Aggie said. "I hear the train."

Sure enough, they heard the distant chugging and then whistle of the train.

"That would be the twelve forty coming in from Grand Haven," Harmen said.

"I wonder what shape the trestle is in," Mrs. Flikkema mused.

"Burnt," Harmen answered promptly. "Burnt to the ground. There's a big gap where it used to be. Don't worry, Grand Haven, Grand Rapids, they know about the fire. Bad news travels fast. No engineer would rush onto the trestle of a city he knows is burnt."

"Still," Rudy said. "Imagine that—first the city burns down, and then just imagine if the train took a plunge into the river because the trestle burned out." He used his hands to show the imaginary train plunging off the trestle while he made wild, explosive sound effects.

"Would it make noise if it fell off the trestle?" Aggie said. "Or would it just sink in the river and disappear?"

"If that train crashed, it would sound like Satan playing handball with thunder," Harmen answered.

There was an eerie silence as they listened for the train. It quieted down, now, and then was silent.

Satan playing handball with thunder, Lyle thought. That pretty much described the fire itself.

When they rounded the point toward home, Lyle looked eagerly toward the corral. The horses would be thirsty by now. He needed to expand their boundaries again so they could have some fresh grass.

"Do you see the horses?" Lyle asked.

"No," Aggie said.

"My eyesight isn't what it could be," Mrs. Flikkema admitted.

Harmen had his back to the shore. As he drew the oars, he strained his neck around to look.

"It's a dark day," he said.

"Could they be loose?" Lyle breathed.

"They're probably just spread out under the trees, eating," Rudy said. "Horses blend in."

"Scarlet!" Lyle called, "Heer-re Scarr-let!" But there was no response. All he could hear was the water dripping off Harmen's oars as he suspended them in the air, listening. When there was no answering call, no sounds of horses snuffling, snorting, or moving, Harmen suddenly dug them into the water again and pulled with hard strokes toward shore.

On shore, Rudy and Lyle jumped over the gunwales of the rowboat together, one from each side, and ran toward and around the enclosure, looking for the horses in the trees. Surely, they would be nearby grazing. They had to be there. Lyle had the feeling he was seeing past them, over the obvious. But then, how could you miss seeing a horse?

"The bridles are gone," Rudy finally said.

Lyle looked over at where Rudy stood.

"Weren't they right here? Isn't this where they were under the boat?"

"*Ja*," Lyle said, his heart sinking. He dug through the harnesses, and, sure enough, there wasn't a bridle left.

"Somebody took the horses, then," Harmen said. "Let's see which way they went."

Sure enough, there was an opening in the corral and a wide cut-up swath of tracks heading east through the forest along the lake.

"Toward the train," Harmen said.

"More than one somebody," Mrs. Flikkema said. "More like five people. One per horse, I'd say."

Lyle glanced across the lake at Holland where the smoke was thin but heavy—more like a light fog. Then it hit him: he had lost everything. His house, his bed tucked into the wall by the fireplace, the archway between the dining room and the stairway where he remembered his mother's face behind a sheet.

He was suddenly furious. Furious at the fire. At Mrs. Flikkema and Harmen for taking him out in the boat when he should have stayed. At anybody who thought they could just help themselves to what they thought they needed.

He ran along the path of hoof prints, so angry that even his vision changed; the edges of everything he saw turned white-hot and seemed to slip out from under him.

Then his legs turned rubbery in collusion with his treacherous vision. He landed in a heap of dead fall. He lay there, his sobs coming out in angry, coarse gasps.

FOURTEEN

The Four-Four-O Up from Chicago

"At least you'll have something in your bellies before you follow them," Mrs. Flikkema said. Lyle stared miserably into the pale flames licking away at the damp sticks piled on their tiny cooking fire. He could hardly trust his voice to come out even.

"Why did they have to take Scarlet, too?" He stabbed a stick into the fire. He struggled for a moment as his fish slipped sideways on his stick. His stomach hurt. Mrs. Flikkema's bread had run out the night before, and this was their first meal of the day.

"They wouldn't have realized she was your horse," Mrs. Flikkema said. "I suppose they assumed they were all Mr. Boone's," she added. "In fact, maybe it was Mr. Boone himself who took the horses."

"Now we don't get any milk for breakfast," Aggie added.

Lyle had never roasted a fish on a stick before, and he was so hungry he kept burning his tongue when he tried eating it. Coals would have been better than the hot flames of the new fire, but nobody wanted to wait long enough for the flames to turn to coals.

"Surely now that it's rained, everyone's going to be heading into town to see what's left, I suppose," Mrs. Flikkema said. "And to find each other." She looked at Lyle.

"You could all come across the lake with us in the rowboat instead of following the horses," Harmen offered. "They're bound to reach Mr. Boone eventually. Then you'll get your Scarlet back."

Lyle stared at his fish. "I don't want to leave her with strangers," he said.

"I want to find Father and Winny," Aggie said.

"So do I," Rudy said. "And we'll need Scarlet to do that. We don't even know where Father and Winny are. They could be all the way to Grand Rapids by now."

"You kids have relatives in Grand Rapids?" Mrs. Flikkema asked.

"*Ja*. But Uncle Egbert's in Zeeland; that's closer." Lyle hoped they wouldn't have to go to Grand Rapids. That was a long day's drive.

"Even if we find her, we can't all ride Scarlet at once," Aggie said.

Lyle looked around at Rudy and Aggie. "Sure we can," he said. "Three of us—that's not too many, really, seeing how small Aggie is. Pieter and I and some friends had five on her before." He smiled remembering their contest to see how many children could pile onto one horse.

"Well, then I get to be in front," Aggie said.

"I wonder where we'll all go," Harmen said. "Jenny doesn't know who to impose on, with five kids."

"Oh, relatives." Mrs. Flikkema laughed. "Jan or Pieter, one of them will have us."

Lyle took his eyes off his fish to look at her. The laughing was real, he decided. He looked at Harmen, who was also giving Mrs. Flikkema a funny look.

"We don't know what's burned, yet," Harmen reminded her. "Jan or Pieter might not be any better off than we are."

"Ha, ha. I know, it's just that—" she paused to wipe at her eyes, "don't you think it's funny, saying, oh, we'll just drop in on them for a few years?"

"*Nee!*" Harmen said. He laughed a little too.

"I know, I know," Mrs. Flikkema said. "It's not funny. But the Lord provides, doesn't He? He sure does provide." Then she neatly pulled her fish off the stick, and in a crisper tone of voice, added, "You children better not dawdle, now, you hear? If you're going to catch up with Scarlet, you've got to get on your way. I'll tell you what. Pile all the harnesses together and we'll put my leaky old boat over them; that way they'll stay in decent shape for Mr. Boone."

Mr. Boone. Lyle groaned. He had thought that Mr. Boone was going to like him now. Mr. Boone was supposed to find him diligently tending to his horses and know what a hero he'd been. But he didn't have Mr. Boone's horses after all.

You don't even like Mr. Boone, a little voice in his head said as he imagined Mr. Boone's hound dog face.

I know, he answered himself. *But I want him to like me.*

"You take one of the blankets with you in case you have to spend the night out again."

"We'll be with Father and Winny by tonight," Rudy said. "You better keep them; you've got all the grandchildren to think about."

"I wouldn't hear of it," Mrs. Flikkema insisted. "If I'm going to watch you walk off on your own, you're at least going to be carrying one of my good wool blankets."

Lyle pushed the last chunk of fish into his mouth, then took his turn to hug Mrs. Flikkema and Harmen goodbye.

"The horses shouldn't be hard to follow," Harmen repeated. "Looks like they're just following along the edge of the lake. If they turn the other way, though, if they don't head back to Holland, you quit following them," he added. "You hear?"

"Yes," Rudy said. "If they take off into the deep dark North, we won't go there."

Harmen pounded Rudy and Lyle on the backs and gave Aggie a kiss on the cheek. "Thanks for taking care of Ma," he said.

He was right about the horses. Five horses going through the woods left plenty of tracks. Not clear hoof prints exactly, but a churned-up trail of kicked leaves and debris. Lyle even found a twisted horseshoe caught on a tree root. He tried to pull the nails out of the holes but couldn't do it with his bare hands. He hung the shoe over his pocket as it was, nails and all. Then they went on, kicking through the heavy leaves that sent up a strong, autumn odor of damp compost. It was a nice change from smoke.

The horse tracks did turn away from the lake eventually. Or they stayed straight east, Lyle realized, and it was the shore that curved. Anyway, the forest was deep and dark. High above them the last few tight-clinging leaves rattled. When the wind blew the clouds away from the sun, momentarily, the light streaked in a crisscrossing pattern through the trees.

"Are there wolves, here?" Aggie asked.

"No," Lyle said, hoping he was telling the truth.

Aggie slipped her hand into Lyle's from time to time, or into Rudy's, depending on who she was closest to. When she had dropped Monkey for the third time, Lyle stopped and used his string to tie Monkey around her waist.

"Now he's in a rucksack," Lyle told her.

"I wish you could put me in a rucksack," Aggie said. "I'm tired."

"You want to ride piggyback?" Lyle asked her.

She nodded, but Rudy volunteered to take her instead. "Just for a little while," he said, and gave Lyle Mrs. Flikkema's blanket to carry before he hoisted her up.

Lyle never realized how heavy a blanket could be, or how scratchy. He tried draping it over his neck until his neck itched, and carrying it folded under his arm, until his arm itched. Rudy took it back after a while, and even Aggie carried it once, but all its edges and corners kept trailing on the ground and getting under her feet. For a little while, Lyle and Rudy figured out how to make it into a sling and carry Aggie in it, like a hammock, between them. She giggled, but Lyle wished they had left the blanket behind.

It wasn't long after their second rest that Lyle heard the unmistakable noise of people gathered.

"It's the train," Rudy said. "*Ja*, I'm sure of it."

Before Lyle even saw the train, he could smell it; he could smell the hot, oily smell of the engine. At last, they came through into a clearing. To the left, the railroad tracks cut a swath through the trees, and to the right, the train at a standstill—first the engine, then two passenger cars, three box cars and a caboose. People swarmed up and down the length of it. The horses—Scarlet and Mr. Boone's horses—had gathered around a few piles of hay that someone had thrown from a boxcar.

"They're here!" he shouted.

"Maybe Father and Winny are here, too," Rudy said.

Lyle ran toward the horses, Rudy and Aggie following. He wrapped his arms around Scarlet's neck. Her coat was rough where she'd been sweating, but she was already cooling down.

Rudy was more interested in the steam engine now that they'd found the horses.

He whistled. "It's the new four-four-O General; would you just look at that."

"They rode them hard," Lyle said.

"It's the engine the fire crew was talking about, just up from Chicago," Rudy said. "She's brand new."

Lyle did look, and he realized it was an engine he hadn't seen before. He was used to the older one with the wide, funnel-like smoke stack on the front. This engine was slimmer with a tall, thin smokestack that didn't widen until the very top. He tried to think of the name of the old one.

"I like The President better," Aggie said.

The President—that was it.

"This one's a wood burner," Rudy said. "Weighs over 65,000 pounds."

Lyle liked steam engines, too—in a way. He liked the way the body was so black and thin and cylindrical, and the smoke stacks so big. For today, anyway, he only knew the train made a great backdrop for the horses—horses he was overjoyed to see.

"I thought they only burned coal," Aggie said. Then she tugged Rudy's sleeve. "Come on, Rudy," she said, so Rudy finally looked around, twirling his cap.

It was easy to tell the people who had come in on the train from the people who had escaped from the fire. The people from Grand Haven looked sympathetic in a rosy, bustling way, but the people from Holland only looked tired, Lyle thought. He saw somebody with their hair singed, and somebody else with their pant legs singed. Not to mention that they looked like they'd slept in their layers of oddly matched clothes.

"You stay with Aggie so she can sit down a minute," Rudy told Lyle. "I'll look for Father."

"*Ja*, all right. Where do you want to meet, by the horses?" Lyle asked.

Rudy nodded, then lumbered away. Aggie didn't wait but sat down on the ground right where she was. They both looked up when a loud, high wolf whistle came from a little farther up the train. Someone had gotten up on a crate and was gesturing in long swooping motions for the crowd to draw near.

"Come on," Lyle told Aggie, and he took her hand to pull her up to her feet again. "Let's go see." They followed along as the others bunched themselves together into a crowd. Then Aggie sat back down.

"Just a quick business meeting," the man shouted. "We'll form a committee in charge of handing out supplies. Any nominations?"

"It ought to be rationed," a man called out. "No more grabbing."

Lyle wondered if the person who had stolen the fish had shown up here already, grabbing stuff off the train.

"You want to be on the committee?"

"*Ja*."

"Name?"

"Jenema. Evert Jenema."

"Then I nominate Evert Jenema. Anyone second it?"

"Lyle!" someone hissed, and Lyle turned around.

"Over here," the voice said, and Lyle recognized the voice an instant before he caught sight of Pieter's face.

"*Hallo*," he said, gripping Pieter's hand.

Pieter threw his arms around Lyle in a bear hug, then punched his arm. Lyle smelled smoke and sweat.

"How are you? What happened to you?" they both asked at once.

"We've been camping out near the train tracks," Pieter told him. He gestured toward the backs of his family mixed in with the crowd. "I thought we were going to freeze last night. Have you eaten? There's food on the train. They sent food."

"Who did?" Lyle asked.

"Food and all kinds of other things."

"Who?"

"Just every single person in Grand Haven. Look." Pieter pulled Lyle up to the nearest railroad car and they peered in through the open door.

The car was full of barrels.

"Are the other cars this full?"

Pieter nodded. "One is just barrels of clothes and food; one is hay and grain for livestock. Have you eaten?"

"We had bread and fish. Twice. And milk. But I'm starving"

"You're lucky. We didn't have anything for two days, until now." Pieter rubbed his stomach. "I had roast beef. It was already cut and everything, like someone took it right off their table at dinner time."

"So, they already knew about the fire," Lyle said. Harmen had been right.

"*Ja*, they knew all right. But nobody knew for *sure* they knew until they got here. You should have seen it—men chased the train down with horses."

"Chasing down the train with horses?"

"*Ja*, they were afraid it was going to crash going over the trestle. The trestle is burned to a crisp, you know."

"Really! That's why they took the horses!"

"Jan Bronkema was one of them. He said they were Mr. Boone's livery horses that some kids saved."

"That was us!" Lyle told him. "We had the horses corralled up down the lake, and somebody took them all. They took Scarlet, too, and I was mad." He could still feel the heat from that anger. "I'm still mad," he added.

"No," Pieter said. "Really? You're the ones, then? You should talk to that reporter over there. He's writing down everything." He pointed to a man with a name tag pinned to his shirt, scrawling down notes. "See? He's from the Grand Rapids Daily Eagle."

Lyle could imagine reading about himself in the headlines: "Boy Rescues Horses and Saves Train From Becoming Handball of Satan!" He'd like Winny to see that one.

Pieter turned his hat around backwards. "Hey, did you see that engine?" he asked.

"Yeah, Rudy about fell off his shoes when he saw it. He knows every little thing about it and it's the first time he's even seen it. He's probably in it right now, instead of looking for Father and Winny, like he said."

"Where are they, anyway?" Pieter asked.

"I don't know. We got separated. When I saw this crowd, I thought they might be here."

Pieter shook his head. "*Nee*, I don't think so."

"Want to help me find Rudy?" Lyle asked him.

Pieter didn't even answer. He helped pull Aggie to her feet again and held her other hand as they headed for the horses.

They ran into Rudy who was talking to one of the shopkeepers from downtown.

The shopkeeper's face lit up.

"A baby? Just a little one?"

"You saw her?" Lyle was suddenly too scared to hope. "Where?"

"Move on up, two, three cars. I saw a lady getting a bite to eat. Had the baby wrapped up and tied right against her. Just a tiny little thing."

Rudy, Lyle, Pieter and Aggie made their way along the cars together, and Lyle's heart sank when he saw that it wasn't Winny with the baby. This woman was older and had other children crowded around her too.

They peered into the woman's arms at the baby.

The woman looked up and smiled.

"How old is he?" Lyle asked.

"Two weeks. Imagine being only two weeks old and having your house burn down."

Or one hour old, Lyle thought. Or one minute.

The woman stroked her baby's cheek and moved away.

"So, there you are," a voice said. It was the man in the moccasins whom they had met at the fish fry yesterday. Mr. Grootenhuis.

"Sorry for taking your horses without a word. We looked but couldn't find you."

Lyle didn't answer. He couldn't think of what to say, but Aggie could.

"We were extremely upset," she said primly.

"We were worried about the train."

"Pieter says you chased it down," Lyle finally said, glancing at Pieter. He wished he had thought of chasing it himself. Even if it didn't need chasing down.

"*Ja.* We had a gallop alongside the train. But Mr. Pieterson, he's the engineer, he says they were already slowing down for the trestle. They weren't going to rush headlong into a burned city."

"Not with the new four-four-0 General," Rudy said.

"And not with fifty lives on board, and cars of supplies," Mr. Grootenhuis corrected. "Say, you said these are Mr. Boone's horses, *Ja?*"

"*Ja,*" Lyle looked at him.

"Well, the trestle's burned out, and we're going to get the supplies to the other side. We'll be needing these horses if you wouldn't mind telling Mr. Boone if you see him. I'm sure he'd want them put to a good cause."

"We'll just take our own horse, Scarlet," Rudy spoke up.

Mr. Grootenhuis tipped his hat at them and left, and Lyle found Scarlet's bridle lying in the boxcar next to the hay.

FIFTEEN

The Underground Organ, Again

Lyle could feel Scarlet's every step—her back feet steps, that is—right through her hips. He rode behind Rudy, riding behind Aggie. He leaned back and petted her red rump as they rode.

As they came out of the swamp, off the corduroy path, Lyle could see the blackened remains of a few houses along the top of the rise, but when Scarlet had scrambled up the incline, the wide-open view took his breath. Even with Aggie and Rudy in front of him on Scarlet, he shivered.

Trees and houses should have blocked his view. But instead, he could see all the way through—over—what used to be Holland. The trees were gone—all the big old shade trees that had lined the streets and stood between the town and the swamp. There was no question if Grandfather, Moses, or the Lightning Tree were left.

Except for the occasional uprights and charred timbers leaning against each other, the fire had leveled the houses, so what was left seemed short, black, and blighted.

Scarlet slowed down, moving cautiously. She had been hurrying toward home, the way any horse does, but now she hesitated. It didn't look like home to Lyle either. It didn't look like any place he'd seen before in his life.

"There's too much nothing here," Aggie said. "I don't like it.

Lyle tightened his arms around her, not knowing what to say.

"The pillar church is still there," Aggie eventually added as Scarlet picked her way forward again.

The church was the first landmark Lyle recognized. It wasn't his church, but it was a church, and he was glad to see it. It looked more grey than white, though.

Scarlet moved cautiously down the path and onto River Street.

"This is River Street, isn't it?" Lyle asked. Everything looked so different, it was hard to be sure these were his own streets in his own town.

"I think so," Rudy answered.

The eeriest thing that Lyle saw was the people. They wandered up and down the streets and rooted around in the heaps of rubble that used to be their homes. There were people with their arms thrown about each other, just standing there, leaning into each other like trees. A few dug and sorted with the burned-off ends of boards.

"Watch out," Aggie said.

A man with a pot belly and a grey beard chased a teenage boy toward them. The boy had a loaded burlap sack thrown over his back, dodging along the street and through the ashes of a house to get away.

"You dig in your own wreck, not mine!" the man shouted after him.

The boy was farther away now, and the man stopped, his face red.

"The thief," he fumed. He looked right at the children on the horse as he muttered. "Scavenging through people's pain, that's what he's doing. What little bit anyone's got left, he helps himself to." Then he turned away.

Lyle shuddered.

"A looter," Rudy said. His voice came out as cracked and strange as the scene itself.

"Let's find our house," Aggie said, "before anybody loots it."

They counted the crossroads along Ninth Street to be sure they turned onto Market Street. Then, on the corner, they saw two men and a woman standing around a big hole in the ground.

"What are they doing?" Aggie asked. "Are they looting?"

Lyle could see them digging and leaning over something heavy. They used a few boards as pry bars but couldn't get whatever it was out of the ground.

"The organ!" Lyle exclaimed.

The man with a big beard looked approvingly up at them.

"A big strapping boy, now, that's what we need," he said to Rudy. He looked at Scarlet and seemed to reconsider. "Or the horse. She could pull this blooming instrument out of this hole."

"Not in one piece," the man's wife said. "Let the boys help. You boys willing to help?"

Lyle was already slipping off Scarlet's back. Rudy landed heavily beside him. "Stay right there and hang onto Scarlet, all right?" Rudy told Aggie.

With their knees bent all the way to the ground, Lyle and the woman shared one corner of the organ. Rudy, the bearded man, and the woman's brother each took one of the other corners.

The man counted to three, said,

"Heave," and with a unanimous grunt, they suddenly had the organ hanging in the air above the hole.

"Move her my way," the bearded man said.

Then the organ was on the ground again, and the woman unwrapped the rug from around it.

Lyle looked into the hole, remembering the first night with Mrs. Flikkema, how he'd told his story about the organ playing under the ground. It was silly, he knew. Childish. But he still liked the idea. The only thing in the hole was some loose dirt and a few pieces of fuzz from the carpet.

"Does it still work?" Aggie called from up on Scarlet. Lyle was glad she asked because, now, more than anything, he wanted to hear the organ play.

"*Ik weet 't*," the man said. He didn't know.

"Give it a try," someone urged. A couple of people had come to see what was going on.

"She can play it. I can't," the man said, as if he didn't care one way or the other, as if it were completely up to his wife. He just didn't want to know any more bad news, Lyle thought. But the woman wasn't as scared. She whooshed her skirt to straighten it beneath her, then sat at the bench. Her feet began to pump the pedals, and she lifted her hands above the keyboard. Lyle heard a grating sound.

The woman stopped pumping. "Grit in the pedals," she said. "Evert, can you see to that?"

Her husband knelt under the narrow keyboard, threaded a handkerchief past the hinge pin, and sawed back and forth with it. Then he blew hard.

"Best I can do for now," he said. "Try her again."

"What do you want to hear?" his wife asked. She poised her hands in the air. The pedals sounded better this time; Lyle only heard the whooshing of compressed air. She didn't wait for an answer.

A familiar chord rang into the air. The woman and her brother began to sing the Doxology. Even her husband, squatting on the ground with his handkerchief between his fingers, stood up. Lyle, Aggie, and Rudy all sang too.

Praise God from whom all blessings flow.
Praise Him all creatures here below.
Praise Him above ye heavenly host.
Praise Father, Son and Holy Ghost.

Then the man with the beard started to clap, and Lyle joined in. But when the woman playing the organ said "Amen," Lyle stopped clapping in case it was the wrong thing to do. You never clapped in a church, and it did suddenly feel church-like. He felt thankful and full of awe all at once for no reason he could think of except for being alive.

A silence followed, and just when Lyle wondered what would happen next, Rudy said,

"I'll play one. If you don't mind."

The woman flipped her skirt and stepped away from the bench.

"Of course," she said. "It would be an honor." The way she said it Lyle knew she knew of Rudy's piano playing. Everyone seemed to know.

Rudy plopped down at the bench. His face looked especially noncommittal, so Lyle expected to hear something astonishing. He was right. The organ didn't have the crisp, quick sound of a piano, of course, but it could make chords that came straight out of heaven. They came straight out of the forest; the sounds Rudy played reminded Lyle of the big old trees they'd just come from, the white pines and oaks that cast such big shadows they made Aggie ask about wolves.

Rudy's feet kept the pedals going, and his hands ran from one chord to the next, all his fingers spread out as they lifted and landed in some new configuration of sound that swelled louder and grander, as if the new steam engine were getting closer. Then, if his music were a train, it was on its way past, the chords getting smaller, softer, turning into the sweet sounds of a lullaby. And Lyle was thinking about Winny again. Rudy was too, because he stood up, rubbed the freckles on his nose and said,

"Thank you. We better get going, looking for our folks."

"*Dank u veer*," the man said. "That was worth burying her for."

"That was worth digging her up for, you mean," his wife added.

"That too. Now you listen here," the man said. "We're taking her to the church, so if you need a place to play, you come right on over."

"Okay, thanks," Rudy said. He moved to Scarlet's head and walked beside her as they started down the street again. "Let's go home," he said.

SIXTEEN

Mr. Boone, Again

Behind them, someone started playing hymns again, and the hymns became fainter as the children got closer to what must have been their own driveway.

"Look." Aggie pointed.

Lyle was afraid it would be the kid with the burlap sack, rummaging through people's ashes. But it was a figure and a horse standing in what he supposed was his own yard.

"Is that Father and Red?" Rudy asked.

"I don't know." Lyle squinted his eyes to see more clearly. "Anyway, it's not Red." Then Scarlet whinnied, and the other horse answered.

The man turned toward them, but it was Mr. Boone and not their father. He was riding one of the livery horses: Old King Cole. Lyle realized he stood in his own yard. It was hard to tell one yard from the other with few landmarks.

For an instant, Lyle thought Mr. Boone might be about to stomp at them or shoo them away, but he didn't. He just tipped his hat at them instead. His jowls hung down, and the bags under his eyes were dark, so he looked more than ever like the basset hound he always reminded Lyle of. He had the reins in his good right hand, and the hook rested on the pommel of the saddle.

"*Hallo,*" Rudy said.

Lyle felt suddenly too shy to talk. Ashamed because he didn't have the horses after all of that. Old King Cole and Scarlet pulled at their reins to nuzzle noses.

"Hey there, whoa now, King," Mr. Boone said.

"Stand back, here."

"Whoa, Scarlet," Lyle said.

"We saved your horses," Aggie told him. Her voice came out high and thin, though, so Mr. Boone didn't catch it.

"What's that, Missy?" he asked. "Speak up."

"We saved your horses."

He stared at them. Glared, really.

"The horses burned up in the fire," he said. "I was at the Graafscaap fire and couldn't get back."

"We saved your horses," Aggie repeated, louder this time.

"You're pulling my leg," he finally said. He looked from each of their faces to the next, then gave Old King Cole's neck a swipe.

"Which horses?"

"Queenie, Tulip, Satin—" Aggie hesitated.

"And Jack," Lyle jumped in.

"Where are they, then, if you saved them?"

"Mr. Bos took them." Lyle nodded his head toward where the portrait gallery used to be. "You know, Mr. Bos. He and Mr. Bronkema, Jan Bronkema, Mr. Grootenhuis and I don't know who else. They're going to use them to bring supplies from the train across the swamp."

"You're not pulling my leg?"

"No," Lyle said. Then he remembered something. He took the horseshoe that was still hanging out one side of his bulging pocket, suddenly glad to be rid of the heavy thing. He held it out to show Mr. Boone while he gently scratched the place where the nails had been poking him.

"I'll be," Mr. Boone said. He took the shoe and turned it over between his one good hand and the hook on the other. "Looks like he clipped it off with a back hoof. That'd been Jack; he's got such an over-stride." He looked at Scarlet. "I saw you'd got your mare back."

Lyle nodded.

"So, your Father must still have Red."

"I guess so," Rudy answered. "We're looking for him; we got separated."

"Well, if your Father's got Red, that makes Scarlet mine, now, doesn't it?" he asked.

Lyle gulped. He frowned. "We need to keep Scarlet so we can find Father."

"A deal's still a deal. He swapped horses with me; so, Scarlet's mine until your filly's weaned."

With sudden hopelessness, Lyle knew it was true. Though it had felt good to find Scarlet this afternoon and ride off with her, this time it wouldn't be so easy. He didn't know why they'd had to run into Mr. Boone first of all people.

"Come on, Aggie," Rudy said. Rudy held his arms up to her, and she landed on the ground.

"Is getting your hand cut off by the train, is that why you don't like children?" Aggie asked.

Rudy rolled his eyes up at the sky.

"Ha. Is that what you kids tell each other? Cut off by the train?"

"Didn't you?" Aggie asked. "And then that makes you mad and you chase children away?"

"Now what would having a bad hand have to do with kids? No one worse than a kid for coming around to pet horses, and then they get stepped on or bit, and there I am to blame. All because a kid comes snooping. Kids and horses, they don't mix. And their mothers are always mad at me."

"So, it's not because of your hand?"

"How did you say the train cut my hand off, again?" he asked.

She hesitated. Lyle finally helped her out.

"You got your foot caught and fell, and the train ran over your hand," he said. "Cut it right off. Isn't that right?"

"Well, it's a whole lot more interesting reason than sugar," he said, and Lyle could hardly believe it, but he was smiling.

"Sugar!" Aggie said.

"Sugar diabetes, and not the kind that makes me sweet." He laughed at his own joke. Then he cleared his throat. "You're the horse-crazy one, aren't you?" he asked Lyle.

Lyle shrugged. Losing Scarlet twice in one day was too much. He didn't look at Mr. Boone.

"You want a job?" Mr. Boone asked.

"What?" This time Lyle did look up.

"You're good with horses. Looks like I've got a bunch of them left, and I've got no barn, no corrals, and nothing to feed them. You want a job helping me out, or not?"

Lyle couldn't believe his ears. He couldn't believe Mr. Boone would take Scarlet away and offer him a job in the same breath. Lyle looked at Rudy, who, as usual, looked noncommittal. Aggie stared at Mr. Boone, though.

"Well, the first thing you can do, if you want, is take care of Scarlet for me. I've got nowhere to keep her for now. So, you hang onto her."

Lyle started to breathe again. "Thanks," he said, but Mr. Boone had turned his back already and was mumbling on.

"I've got a lot of arrangements to make if I'm going to keep my business going, and somebody's going to have to take care of the horses."

"Okay. *Ja.* Sure," Lyle finally said. "*Dank U zeer.* I'll work hard, I promise."

"I can't be spending all my time looking after the horses when I've got to put together a whole new livery, somehow." He picked up King's reins. "Giddup," he said.

He rode out of the driveway and Lyle rested his hand gratefully on Scarlet's withers, twirling a strand of her flaxen mane between his fingers. He stared after Mr. Boone. He couldn't tell if Mr. Boone was letting him keep Scarlet to be nice, or because he really needed the help.

Rudy raised his eyebrows as Mr. Boone rode off.

"Your lucky day," he said. "Look, I have an idea. I want to ride Scarlet over to the church. There were a bunch of people there, and somebody must know something about Father and Winny."

"Okay, sure," Lyle said, and when Aggie said she wanted to go too, Lyle helped both Rudy and Aggie onto Scarlet's back again. He watched them ride off, then stepped over the thick foundation of stone that outlined the house.

He would be working for Mr. Boone. He could hardly believe it. No more watching all those horses from next door, but actually feeding and grooming them himself. It wouldn't matter if Mr. Boone did have Scarlet over there if Lyle could take care of her.

He poked with his toe at an ice box. He picked up a long rod of sooty iron and turned it over in his hands. It was the poker from the fireplace. He raked through the ashes with it. On one end of the house, one of the brick chimneys still stood about halfway up; the other had fallen over and collapsed into the ashes. He kicked some of the bricks aside.

He didn't know what he was hoping to find, but somehow, he wanted to at least look. Everyone else in town seemed to be doing the same thing.

He picked up a small round metal object and held it experimentally to his nose. It had the same acrid smell as everything else around, but the familiarity of the gesture brought home exactly what it was: Winny's sniff box. All the ladies at church had them—little metal containers holding perfume-soaked sponges. Winny's was especially lovely. Hers was silver—an engraved potbellied container with a hinged lid. Father had given it to her. Lyle polished some of the black off on his pants until he got down to some streaky brown and blue, then slipped the sniff box into his pocket.

By the time Rudy and Aggie arrived back on Scarlet, Lyle had rescued a small pile of items. The fire poker was one. There was also a flour sifter, a ceramic urn, and Winny's sewing machine with one of the knobs and the needle melted off. Lyle wondered how the tin sifter and the sniff pot had survived the heat while it half melted the sewing machine and the ice box.

Rudy didn't know, and he was too full of information to ponder it. He didn't even get off Scarlet.

"I talked to Mr. Keppel at the church," he told Lyle. "He said to try looking at the school. At Hope. It didn't burn down, and a lot of people are camped there. Let's go."

"Hope is still standing?" There were several big buildings on the grounds of Hope Preparatory School. It seemed too good to be true that the school was still intact.

"He said it's all spared."

Aggie leaned out from behind Rudy. "Remember how Mr. Post was watering down his house? With buckets? They said that's why Hope School didn't burn down. Mr. Post's house wouldn't burn, and that split the fire in two."

"Anyway, come on," Rudy said again. "He said to start looking there. And if not, that a lot of people went to Dominie VanRaalte's place too." Dominie VanRaalte had a great big house outside of *de stad*.

Lyle left the big items tucked near the foundation of the house, and then he walked alongside Scarlet. He held up the little pot to show Rudy and Aggie, but when Aggie reached out to take it, he quickly put it back in his pocket. "You might drop it," he said.

She was just opening her mouth to protest when they saw Mrs. Cox in the passenger seat of a road cart, her black midwife's bag in her lap. A man was driving, and she sat next to him, leaning easily against the back of the seat.

"Mrs. Cox," Lyle and Rudy called in unison. "Wait!"

"*Hallo*," she called to them.

"We're looking for Winny and Father," Lyle called. He had to run to keep up because the man driving didn't stop the horse.

"They're at your Uncle Egbert's; didn't you hear?" she asked.

"No! Is she okay? Is the baby okay?"

"We can't stop," she said. "Mrs. Jenema needs me."

"But are they okay?" Lyle asked.

"She's doing fine," Mrs. Cox called cheerily over her shoulder.

Lyle ran faster to keep alongside her, wishing he were the one on Scarlet. "What about the baby?"

"Fine. Strong. Kicking."

"Boy or a girl?"

Mrs. Cox laughed. "Wait and see!" she called. Then Mr. Jenema cracked his whip, and the little bay broke into a spanking trot.

Lyle didn't try to keep up anymore. All he could think now was "fine, fine, fine." Winny was fine. The baby was fine.

"Tell her I'll stop by tomorrow," Mrs. Cox called back to him. "But if you need me sooner, I'll be at Jenema's if I'm not at Hope."

They wouldn't need her again any time soon, Lyle thought, but he just waved and headed back to the others.

"Did you hear that?" he asked.

"We heard," Aggie said.

"Do you think we can get to Uncle Egbert's by dark?" Lyle asked.

"We can try," Rudy answered.

SEVENTEEN

Winny

When Rudy, Lyle, and Aggie arrived at Uncle Egbert's, the sun had already set, and they rode past his two-room log house to his barn by the late dusk light. Lyle could see the first star of the night, but he was too tired to wish for anything but sleep.

"You two go in," he told Rudy. "I'll take care of Scarlet." The truth was, he was half afraid to go in. Afraid to see Winny now, after all this time. Too shy to tell the story of everything that happened.

Then Cookie whinnied from inside Uncle Egbert's barn. Scarlet answered, her voice full-throated, moving up and down the scale. She sounded as grateful to be reunited with Cookie as Lyle felt at being almost home. Almost-home, he told himself, was anyplace Father and Winny were.

Still, he dawdled in the barn getting velvety filly kisses from Cookie. Then he pumped Scarlet a bucket of water and looked around in the half-dark while she drank. Red and Cookie were already in the only two standing stalls. The team of oxen and a milk cow had the run and a small corral in the yard. He finally tied Scarlet to a post along the wall, then climbed the ladder through the dark square that led to the loft.

He was groping around for hay when he heard the barn door creak open. The square of the trap door brightened with the alternating shadows and light of a swinging lantern.

"Lyle?" he heard. It was Uncle Egbert.

"Up here," Lyle called.

He heard the creaking as Uncle Egbert started up the ladder. First the lantern appeared at the edge of the trap door, and then Uncle Egbert's shiny bald head and thick golden beard poked into view. The light flickered across his face. As usual, his head looked like the wide end of a chicken egg. *He should spell his name with two G's*, Lyle thought. *Eggbert.* He smiled.

"Hi there," Uncle Egbert said.

"*Hallo.*"

"Finding what you need?"

"I was just getting Scarlet some straw."

Uncle Egbert heaved himself through the square and into the loft to gesture with his lantern.

"Hay to the south," he said. "Straw to the north."

Uncle Egbert's beard reminded Lyle of the armload of straw he had. His face was broad and calm, his nose small and freckled like Rudy's. Lyle wondered if Rudy would end up with a bald, egg-shaped head, too. He yawned.

"Tuckered out?" Uncle Egbert asked.

"*Ja.*"

He followed Uncle Egbert down the ladder again, and together they spread the straw around Scarlet's feet. They put the hay close under her nose even while she pulled it out of their arms.

"That should do it," Uncle Egbert said. "Come here," and he held his arms out wide.

Lyle pressed himself against Uncle Egbert's potbelly.

"I thought your ma and pa were going to drive me to drink if you three didn't show up soon. All I heard was where you might be, what you might be doing, how they were going to find you." His smile pushed his beard wide as he loosened his grip on Lyle. "Now get yourself on in the house so they can see you with their own eyes."

They took the path to the house.

Father and Winny were waiting with the door open, and even when Father caught Lyle in a crushing embrace, Lyle twisted around to double check the surprising sight. For a second, he'd thought that Winny still looked pregnant.

But when he turned around, he knew for sure she was still pregnant. The first thing he saw was her huge belly, and the first thing he thought was that it wasn't over. He might have found her only to lose her again.

She opened her arms wide, and he turned into them.

"Winny!" he said. He wrapped his arms around her from the side, moving into the warmth of everything he loved about Winny.

Then Aunt Reka and Uncle Bernard with his wavy black beard were pulling him away from Winny to hug him too.

"If you were my kids, I'd have skinned you alive," Aunt Reka said. "Jumping out like that. *Dank God* you're back."

He kissed Aunt Reka's cheek anyway.

"Winny?" Lyle said again. "I thought you already had the baby. I thought you had it and you were all right. How could you not have had it yet?"

"That was a false alarm," she said. "Just false labor, they call it."

He groaned.

"I know," she said.

"But you were in bed and everything when we left. Remember? I thought you were having the baby."

"Yes. No. See, Mrs. Cox says that a bad case of nerves can bring on false labor—you know, the fire. All that running around I did. So, she made me drink all the water I could stand and lie still for a few hours. It worked." She took hold of his shoulders and backed him away so she could look him in the face. "So where have you been?" she asked.

"Everywhere," he said, too full of renewed dread about Winny to even think about it.

"Everywhere," his father boomed. "That's what I heard. Mr. Boone's barn, the swamp, the lake, the woods, the train. Where haven't you been?"

Lyle didn't know how to answer that question, but he didn't have to because Uncle Egbert cleared his throat from where he was still standing outside waiting to get through the door. Winny and Father made way for him, and then Uncle Bernard and Aunt Reka made way. Uncle Egbert disappeared through the doorway of the second room and Aggie came out at the same time. Lyle saw that any time anyone moved in this house a chain reaction would happen. If one person went into a room, one had to come out. Probably like in the old days, he thought, when Holland was new, and all the orphans went to live in other people's homes.

Then Aggie crept under Father's arm so that he picked her up and held her on his hip even though her long legs hung down to his knees.

"I've never been so scared in my life," Father said. "The idea of losing all three of you at once..." His voice trailed off and he leaned his head against Aggie. Winny leaned into Aggie too, holding out an arm to Lyle. Lyle tucked himself under it, feeling a surge of well-being. Even so, he couldn't keep from yawning again.

"Where are Sietze and Jenny?" Aggie asked, yawning too.

Winny nodded her head at the closet bed next to the fireplace. Lyle cautiously moved the curtain aside and saw the two sleeping bundles.

"Where is everyone sleeping, anyway?" he asked. The bed that Sietze and Jenny were in was the only bed that he remembered Uncle Egbert having.

"Reka and Bernard with the children," his father said. "Winny and I and Egbert on the floor in the other room. Egbert did a little cleaning in the attic for when you three showed up. Looks like you need to get yourselves there right about now."

Although the attic was small and its ceiling was low, it had a wooden floor. Uncle Egbert just moved two old chairs and a trunk to one side, and then shook out a feather mattress. Lyle had never been so thankful for a bed, even if it was a makeshift one. He fell asleep so quickly, he was hardly even aware of Aggie and Rudy crawling in next to him.

In the morning, the first thing he heard was Winny's voice coming from downstairs. Rudy was next to him still, but Aggie had gone.

"One diaper!" Winny laughed. "One is better than none at all," she said. "*Dank u.*"

Aggie must have given her Monkey's diaper. He thought of the fish dinner they had all had, using that diaper for a plate, and wasn't surprised to hear Winny say that she'd get it washed up.

"Are you awake?" Lyle whispered to Rudy. Rudy stretched beside him and rolled over, eyes open. He propped himself up on one elbow, his broad freckled face on his palm. "Ja," he said. "I am now."

"Do you still have the spoon?"

Rudy produced it from under the corner of the feather mattress. "I was sleeping on it," he said, "until I took it out of my pocket somewhere in the middle of the night."

"Let's go show it to Winny."

Lyle had thought that Winny would be happy, from how she'd laughed over the irony of having only one diaper. When they showed her Rudy's spoon, the watch, and the sniff box Lyle had found, she began to cry. She smiled and, at the same time, tears rolled down her cheeks.

"Oh, this spoon," she said. "I know they weren't anything fancy, really, but they were my grandmother's."

"It's yours. You can have it," Rudy offered.

Winny wiped at her eyes, but her mouth continued to pull in funny directions. Her hands were on the top of her stomach, and Lyle thought for a moment she was talking to her own hands, until he realized she was talking to the unborn baby instead. "Poor little dear," she said. "How am I going to take care of you?" Her mouth completely lost its shape this time before she covered it and gave way to weeping again. Then she put an arm around Lyle and Rudy, pulling them toward her, and Lyle felt relieved that she didn't make them suffer alone.

"At least I have you," she said.

Winny was as afraid of losing the baby as he was of losing her, Lyle thought. He pushed his forehead tightly against hers, squinting his eyes and praying for them both. Then he had an idea.

When Winny had let them go, Lyle pulled Rudy outside.

"I want to get supplies from the train for Winny's baby," he whispered. "Do you think Father will let me go?"

"I don't know, but I heard someone say they were setting up food lines and hand-outs at the church. They're rationing and handing out the supplies from Grand Haven."

It turned out easy for Lyle to get back to town. Breakfast was so slim that Father asked Rudy to go to the church to ask for flour. Uncle Egbert always bought his bread from a neighbor lady who baked once a week, and now that the whole town needed bread, she didn't have enough to go around.

Rudy just pointed his thumb at Lyle, saying,

"He wants to go." So Father let Lyle go instead. Lyle even had use of the surrey.

Lyle stood in the food line first, and when he had the bag of flour and small squares of yeast, he put them in the surrey. Then he looked up and down along the table where a woman was handing out donated clothes.

"What do you need, then?" the woman asked, sizing Lyle up at the same time.

"Oh, it's not for me. I have enough stuff. It's for a baby." *Just in case the baby lived*, he told himself.

"How old?"

"Brand new. Newborn."

"Boy or girl?"

"I don't know yet. He's not even born yet. Or she."

"I know I saw some baby things in here." She dug into the barrel, then pulled out an armload of clothing that was in her way and dumped it on the table. Her arms disappeared back into the barrel again.

Lyle looked at the things on the table. There was the Dutch style of button up trousers with a flap in front and some others that opened right up the middle, instead. He saw a silky blue evening gown with fur trim around the collar and sleeves. There was a mink stole and a black lace petticoat. Lyle looked quickly away.

"Oh, that," the woman said, rolling her eyes. "Just ignore that. I don't know who sent that." Then she pulled out a bundle of white layette items all tied up with a ribbon. "Here we go. Look at this." She undid the ribbon, then rolled the bundle open so the delicate baby-sized items fell out onto the table.

There were several tiny, long nightgowns with drawstrings around the bottom. There was a thick stack of diapers. There was a tiny knit cap and sweater, so small he was sure it wouldn't even fit Aggie's monkey, much less a real live baby. His favorite was a set of soft, slightly stretchy blankets with lace around the edges. There were several tiny booties and matching mittens without thumbs.

He held up a mitten.

"So the baby doesn't scratch himself," the lady told him. "With his own fingernails. Babies do that sometimes."

"Oh," he said.

"Has she got anything else?" the lady asked.

"We've got one diaper." Lyle gestured to the pile. "It looks like a lot. Thank you."

"It won't go far with a newborn baby," the lady said. "But it's a start, isn't it?"

EIGHTEEN

Anders Dirk

When Lyle arrived back with Scarlet and the surrey, his father and Uncle Egbert were waiting to leave with it again.

"Where's everyone else?" Lyle asked. The place was quiet compared to the night before.

"Bernard and Reka took the oxen and the kids back to Graafschap to see what they can see," Uncle Egbert answered. "They're going to meet us at the Pillar Church. Dominie VanRaalte called a citizens' meeting."

"I heard," Lyle said. The lady from Grand Haven handing out the clothes had told him about it.

"I want one of you to stay with Winny," Father added. "She can't go. But if a couple of you want to come along, that'd be fine."

"I'll stay," Lyle said quickly.

"I'll go," Rudy said.

They looked at Aggie. "I'll stay," she said. "It's too full of nothing over there." Her eyes slid sideways, then she blurted out, "People are smoking too many cigars!" She laughed happily at her own joke and even Lyle felt himself smile.

Aggie helped Lyle carry in the things he'd brought from the church. They gave Winny the flour and yeast first, and then Lyle handed her the bundle of baby things.

"It's a layette," he said, watching her face to see what she thought.

She undid the ribbon.

"I know it's not the same as the ones you lost, with the lace," he added, when she didn't say anything.

She was crying again, and she hugged the little blankets to her face. "They're beautiful," she said. "I love them. Thank you."

But she continued to cry.

"Are you okay?" Lyle asked.

"I don't know what's wrong with me," Winny said. "I'm sorry. They're just beautiful; they really are. Thank you." She smoothed her hair back and rubbed her forehead. "I'll get going on the bread; that ought to make me feel better."

"Don't you feel good?" Aggie asked.

"I think it's just…" Her voice trailed off. "I'll just make bread. That'll take my mind off it. Aggie, you can help me."

"I might check the horses, then?" Lyle asked. He was nervous about Winny. She was acting strange, and he didn't know if it would be right to leave or not.

"Sure," Winny said.

"I'll just be right out in the barn," he added. "You can call me."

"All right," Winny said. She gathered measuring cups and bowls.

In the barn, Lyle turned Cookie and Red into the corral so they could exercise while he mucked out their stalls. The oxen were gone, and he didn't think the horses would bother the milk cow. Red merely walked along the edge of the fence, nibbling at the already short weeds and grass she could reach just under the fence. Cookie cantered around, her tail high, darting past Red and bucking in invitation to play.

Lyle had just found Uncle Egbert's wheelbarrow and pitchfork when Aggie came running out of the house, calling him.

"It's the real thing," Aggie gasped. "Hurry up."

Lyle didn't have to ask her what real thing she was talking about. He ran in to find Winny curled on her side on the bed, gasping. There was a puddle on the floor, and Lyle saw that the bed was wet too.

Then Winny took a deep breath and uncurled a little. "My waters broke," she said.

"That's all right," Lyle said. "We can clean it up." He realized at once what a ridiculous thing it was to say, since their problem was a lot bigger than cleaning up. "We'll have to get Mrs. Cox," he added.

"Don't go," Winny said, her voice panicky. She reached her hand out, so Lyle took hold of it.

"Mrs. Cox is supposed to stop by," Aggie said. "Remember? She told us she'd stop by."

Lyle remembered in relief that it was true, but Winny couldn't answer because another pain came over her, and her face went rigid, her breathing suddenly shallow.

Lyle placed Aggie's hand over Winny's. First, he washed from the pitcher and bowl by the sink. Then he stoked up the cooking stove and started heating more wash water.

"Are you okay?" Lyle asked Winny.

"I don't know," she said.

"I don't think we should wait for Mrs. Cox to stop by," Lyle said. "How do we know when she'll get here? It could be too late by then. I'd better go look for her."

"Don't go," Winny said again. "What if I have—I mean. Aggie's too little."

"I could go," Aggie offered. "I could ride Red. It's not that far."

Winny nodded gratefully, so Lyle tucked Aggie's hand over Winny's and raced to the barn to get Red bridled for Aggie. He trotted Red to the house, yelling for Aggie to come out. He boosted her on, not so carefully, he suddenly remembered, as he'd done a few days ago when the fire came.

"Get Father first," he said. "Then Father can go looking for Mrs. Cox."

"Okay," Aggie said.

"Hurry," he demanded. He didn't wait to watch her ride Red out to the road, or even turn to glance at Cookie when he heard her calling from the corral. He just ran into the house to Winny again.

She was whimpering, her voice high and heartbreaking.

"I'm back," he told her. He hadn't known that having a baby hurt that much. Scarlet had made it seem easy when she had Cookie.

Winny turned her head to stare into his face, though he had the feeling she wasn't seeing much. Then finally she relaxed again and became herself for a minute or so.

Between every pain Lyle got a tiny bit done. He searched for the mop and found it, then held her hand again. After the next spell, he mopped the wet spot on the floor. And after the next one, he pulled the wet bedding out from under her, one blanket at a time. He found a short stack of towels and placed one carefully under her to cover the wet spot on the mattress and give her a dry place to lie.

"The skirt of your dress is wet through," he told her. "Do you want to get it off and have a blanket over you, instead?"

They had to wait through one more pain before they could get the skirt off. He was sorry for her, having to show her legs, and he ran up to the attic for Mrs. Flikkema's blanket. It wasn't like there was anything bad about him seeing her legs, he thought. They were like Aggie's, only longer and not all scraped up. But he stretched the blanket over her to make her more comfortable.

"That'll be better," he said.

"Can you bring me some water?" Winny asked.

Lyle pumped the short handle at the sink, letting the water run itself cold before he filled the cup. The hour hand on Uncle Egbert's clock had gone around one full time and, still, no one had come.

When he got back to her side, Winny had another pain. Her eyes were glazed, and she arched against the contraction. Her breath came in short, shallow puffs, as if the air couldn't get all the way to her lungs. Lyle waited till it was over, then handed her the cup and took it away again after she had swallowed several times.

"You're so good to me, Lyle," she said.

"No, I'm not," he answered, alarmed by how grateful she seemed. Water didn't mean anything. She could have as much water as she wanted, and it wouldn't make him good. To really be good, he'd have to ease her pain somehow. Or share it.

"But I would be good, if I could," he added and he prayed, "I'll take half her pain, Lord." But nothing happened. He realized it was too selfish a prayer, only taking half. "I'll take it all," he offered, wondering if he could stand it half as well as Winny could. Still nothing happened except that she got another contraction, obviously all to herself.

"Winny?" Lyle asked her when it was over. Between pains, she didn't seem to mind talking.

She looked up at him, her golden-brown hair rubbing the pillow again.

"I don't have a crush on you," he said. He couldn't keep himself from telling her.

"Sweetheart," she said. She never called him sweetheart. Usually, she saved that for Aggie. "It's okay if you have a crush on me. I think it's really nice."

"But I don't. It's not a crush. I just love you."

"I love you too," she said. She pulled his head toward her in the crook of her elbow.

He turned her hand over in his and began to cry, despite trying not to. Being stoic failed him.

Winny's eyebrows moved up and down as if she were thinking something else, but before she could say it, another pain came. It seemed to sweep her away from him.

He thought of all the times he'd imagined Winny just happening to look out the window and see him doing something heroic. It was supposed to make her suddenly love him more, or something. But now he was the one seeing her do something heroic, instead.

"Here," she finally said, offering him the edge of the blanket to dry his tears.

"Do you think you're going to die?" he asked. There. It was out. He'd said it.

"You mean someday?" she asked.

"Right now," he said. "Having the baby."

"Oh. Like your mother, you mean," she said.

"Uh huh," he said. "When you have one of those pains."

Sure enough, she had another one. He watched her face, wishing she would breathe. Then it was over again.

"You don't die of pain," she finally said. "Besides, I have to prove your father did the right thing marrying an American, now, don't I? Dying would give everyone just too much to talk about."

And that was that. There she was joking, right on her deathbed, sounding like her usual self. Lyle almost smiled.

Then he wondered what had happened to Aggie. He tried to figure in his head just how long it should take her. He should have taken Red and gone himself. He could have galloped—raced like a maniac—and been there in fifteen minutes. Mrs. Cox would be here already.

But he'd have had to leave Winny, and she wanted him here. Wanted him. Even now, he didn't want to leave her for one second. If she lost the baby or something went wrong.... He couldn't bear to think about it. It would be his fault.

Just when Lyle had gotten used to the rhythm of things the way they were, Winny's pains changed. Instead of panting through it like before and whimpering, she suddenly groaned as if she were pushing every breath of air out of her lungs. Her face turned red and momentarily swollen with the strength of her push.

"Are you okay?" he couldn't help gasping when it was over.

"I couldn't help it," she said. "I had to push. I think the baby's coming."

"It's okay," he said. She was having the baby now, Lyle thought. Or else she was dying.

Then the door burst open, and Mrs. Cox came in, saying, "Sounds like I barely made it on time; someone should have come for me." She dropped her bag on the table and pushed the curtain open in front of the bed. Lyle could have kissed her.

"How are you, Winny?" she asked, even as her hands slipped under the blanket. "Lyle, are you here alone?"

He nodded. "Aggie is trying to find Father, who's supposed to find you."

"Looks like you're doing beautifully taking care of things."

"She's about to have the baby," was all he could think to say.

"Can you see to my horse? I left him standing just outside when I heard—"

Lyle slipped outside. The little bay was grazing near the door, his reins fallen under his feet. Lyle leaned into his silky shoulder to shift his weight. He untangled the reins before he led him to the barn. Then, even from inside the barn, he could hear Winny's next shrieking push.

He fumbled to tie the bay in the standing stall, then ran back to the house. He needed to be there with her, knowing every second that she was still alive.

He burst through the door.

Mrs. Cox had helped Winny turn over on her back now, her knees drawn up on either side of her big belly. Her face was wet, rivulets of sweat running into her hair.

Mrs. Cox turned to him. "You'll want to wait in the next room. She's getting really close."

"I'll stay right by her head," Lyle said. "She needs me; I want to be here in case—" He frowned. "To keep her from—"

Mrs. Cox took him by both shoulders, speaking gently.

"Lyle, listen to me. Winny's not dying; she's having a baby, that's all."

"How do you know?" he demanded.

"Because I know. Because the baby is exactly where he ought to be. Because Winny's strong. Because—" Then she interrupted herself. "Do you know why your mother died?" she asked.

He shook his head, but he thought, *because I wanted a little brother or sister.*

"Because that baby was facing the wrong way. He tried to come feet first, and face up to boot, and most babies just can't be born that way. Their head gets stuck, and the mother does everything to push him out, but she couldn't do it. She labored for sixty hours straight. We finally had to pull—"

Winny drowned her out with another loud, shrieking push.

Mrs. Cox turned back to Winny, letting Lyle stay close after all. She helped Winny grasp her own knees, pulling them toward her shoulders as she pushed. Mrs. Cox's hands never left Winny, but she turned her face back to Lyle again, speaking urgently into his ear.

"It was too late for your baby brother—and then it turned out to be too late for your mother, too. But that's not how things are for Winny."

Lyle felt sick, thinking of his mother in this much pain for that many hours. And then dying of it.

"Maybe I shouldn't have told you," she said.

"*Ja*, you should have; it's okay," he said, and he relaxed the muscles in his face, so she would know he was okay and trust him enough to let him stay. She had to know he could take it.

Lyle thought about Mrs. Flikkema's big world she'd talked about. How she said heaven was like the other side. The other side of what? he wondered. The other side of fire? He tried to imagine heaven with its own shoreline, across some lake, or maybe a river. Yes, a river, only it was dark and he couldn't see it clearly. No—not a river, just a stream, he decided. One he could skip a stone across or hop across himself if only it were daylight.

His mother was right on the other side of that stream, and so was little Paul who had tried to be born feet first. Lyle remembered to think of Mrs. Flikkema's five-year-old daughter, too—the one whose voice Mrs. Flikkema still missed when they sang Psalms before eating. She was also on the other side.

"Lyle." Mrs. Cox pressed a blanket into his hands. "Take this and go stand by the stove with it. Hold it out and get it warmed up. Both sides. We're going to need it good and warm."

Then her back was to him again as she went back to coaching, her eyes locking with Winny's and her voice loud.

"Not yet, honey. Wait till the count of five." There was barely a pause and she said, "NOW," and Winny was making another terrifyingly loud noise—louder than all five people earlier that day lifting the organ out of the ground. She was giving birth to an organ, Lyle thought.

Lyle held the blanket as close to the stove as he dared, till he felt his forehead bead with sweat and the back of his hands burn. Then he refolded the blanket and started toasting a new side.

"Push, push, push," the midwife urged, and Winny drowned her out with her huge groan.

Then the door of the house opened again. It was Father and Aggie. It seemed like ages ago that Aggie had left.

"Oh, *God dank* you're here," Father said to Mrs. Cox. "We looked everywhere for you."

Aggie's eyes turned big and scared looking when she heard Winny groan again. She stepped up to the fire next to Lyle.

"It's okay," Lyle told her. "She has to make that sound to push the baby out."

"You're just in time to help," Mrs. Cox told him. "Is there any cord around here? We're going to need a short length of cord."

"In the attic, in my pants pocket, there's a string," Lyle said. Then Lyle reached into his Sunday pants pocket—the ones he was wearing—where he'd transferred Winny's little sniff pot. He handed it to Aggie. "Just keep rubbing it," he said, "for good luck." He thought it would make her feel better even though it didn't have any perfume in it.

She took the little pot, looking appreciatively at it. Then she lay it smoothly on her cheek.

When Father came down with the string, Mrs. Cox dropped it into the pot of simmering water on the stove. "To tie the umbilical cord," she explained.

Lyle had turned and turned and turned the blanket until it was warm and then warm again. His arms ached from holding it out, and yet the baby still didn't come.

"How come it's taking so long?" Lyle asked.

"That's normal," his father said.

"But do you think the baby is stuck? Maybe it won't come out?"

"No. It's normal."

"But Mother—Mrs. Cox said she had to push for too long."

"Your Mother did just fine having Rudy, you and Aggie, didn't she? I know what I'm talking about."

"I can see his head," Mrs. Cox suddenly said. "He's got dark hair," she reported. "Lots of dark hair. Now push push push."

"There it is," she said, "his head. Just rest up a minute before his shoulders."

Anders Dirk, Lyle thought to himself. The baby was going to be Anders Dirk.

But Winny didn't have a choice as she shrieked with one last powerful push, and Mrs. Cox lifted the tiny, wet, red baby into the air.

"It's a girl," she said.

Lyle moved close to her with the blanket. He couldn't take his eyes off the baby. She was hanging in the air on Mrs. Cox's arm, red and wet, all squiggling arms and legs. Then Mrs. Cox landed her gently on Winny's belly, messy as she was. She wasn't Anders Dirk at all, but Leah Marie, the tiniest, wettest, red human being Lyle had ever seen.

"I'll get the string," Mrs. Cox said, "and we'll cut the cord." She dropped her scissors into the boiling water while she fished out the string with a fork. When she had tied the cord in two places, she retrieved the hot scissors, using a towel as a potholder, and clumsily cut the cord between the two knots.

Then Mrs. Cox took the baby to the table and toweled her off. Winny was shaking so hard that her legs wouldn't even lie still. Her teeth chattered and her arms trembled in the air where she held them out toward the baby. "Let me have her," she said in a jarring, trembling way, and even her smile shook and rattled.

"One second, there," Mrs. Cox said. She turned to get the blanket Lyle was holding. "Oh—good and warm. Perfect," she said. She scooped the blanket out of Lyle's arms and landed it over Winny. Then she tucked the baby into Winny's arms under the blanket.

Lyle himself felt the comfort of that warm blanket.

NINETEEN

The Loaf of Bread

When Lyle came up from the barn that evening, he was surprised to see a team of oxen at the hitching post. He peered through the window into the lighted room, and there was Harmen, shaking hands with Uncle Egbert and Father. Already seated at the table, Mrs. Flikkema had a familiar bundle in her arms. She had brought them a loaf of bread, he thought. He was never going to be able to think of her without bread.

"You came!" he exclaimed as he burst through the door.

"Shush, now," Mrs. Flikkema said. "Winny is resting." She made a clucking sound to the bundle in her arms.

Lyle had to take a closer look.

The bundle was Leah Marie in one of the white blankets. She made a tiny sound, a miniature blat like a sheep makes, and Mrs. Flikkema tucked the blanket a little tighter around her. "There, now," she said. Leah Marie was wearing the tiny little outfit from the layette—and it was plenty big.

Lyle laughed. "I thought she was a loaf of bread. I thought you brought us all another loaf of bread."

Mrs. Flikkema smiled too. "Ha," she said. "This time you're glad it's a baby, and not bread." She clucked to Leah again.

"I know," Lyle agreed.

"I see you all found a home," Mrs. Flikkema said.

"They've got a home as long as they need one," Uncle Egbert said. "The whole clan."

"The whole kit and caboodle," Aunt Reka added.

"Kit and caboodle is right," Mrs. Flikkema said. "We've got a kit and caboodle of our own staying at Pieter's, and they already had a kit and caboodle before we ever got there—nine kids of their own, and then we all drop in."

While she talked, Lyle found himself a spot to sit on the floor against Winny's bed since all the chairs were taken. He looked up at Winny. She looked okay except for being extra rosy.

"This will be our incentive to rebuild in a hurry," Father said.

Then Lyle realized that's what the town meeting had been about—whether to rebuild the town. He'd been so taken up with Winny and the birth that he'd never asked about it.

"Everyone?" Lyle asked. "Or just us?"

"The whole town," Father answered. "Everything that burned down. Sixty-four stores, six churches, three printing offices, two tanneries, two banks, two art galleries, let's see—"

"Five saloons and 200 houses," Rudy added. "Plus, boarding houses, docks, sidewalks and shanties."

"And the grist mill with thousands of bushels of wheat," Harmen finished.

"And most of it uninsured or under insured," Father sighed. "But that might be a blessing in disguise, because Chicago burning at the same time is going to send the insurance companies belly up."

"Christians live on faith, not insurance," Uncle Egbert added.

"What did Dominie VanRaalte say?" Harmen asked. "We will rebuild the town with our Dutch tenacity and our American experience."

"And our faith." Uncle Egbert raked his fingers through the curls in his black beard.

"Well, that's how it got started in the first place; no reason we can't do it again," Mrs. Flikkema added. Then she turned to Leah Marie. "Isn't that right?" she asked, her wrinkled face soft and lighted as she stroked Leah Marie's cheek. Then Mrs. Flikkema looked around at the group, her face hardening again as if daring anyone to defy her, but everyone seemed in agreement.

"Mrs. Tolk lost her life," Harmen said. "The poor widow. They found her remains in her house."

The children looked around at each other, gulping.

"All of this loss of property, yet only one life taken. We are so blessed." Mrs. Flikkema gestured for Lyle's father to take Leah, then she held both hands out to Lyle. "You just help me up, here," she told him. "Thatta boy. You boys got good at getting my old bones off the ground these last few days, I'll say that for you."

"You just got here," Aggie protested.

"Somebody else just got here, too," Mrs. Flikkema said, nodding toward Leah. "If we'd have known she was only born today, we wouldn't have come pestering you." She pressed her wrinkled cheek against Lyle's, and he thought how much younger the fire had made her. Imagine that she didn't used to come out of the house, and now she had traveled to Zeeland.

"Mrs. Flikkema?" Lyle asked her at the door.

"What now?" she asked.

Lyle felt too full of the emotion of the day to even stop himself. "Do you believe in Hell?"

Behind him, he felt every single adult listen. It was a touchy question.

Mrs. Flikkema looked at him, too, piercingly, then gave him a slap on the shoulder. "I believe in love, that's what I believe in. Now you take care of your horses and your baby sister," she added.

"I will," he said.

It wasn't until the middle of the night that Lyle first had the baby to himself. He crept down the ladder and into the kitchen. Leah Marie was in an apple box near the fireplace where a small fire still burned. Winny was asleep. Her arm hung down over the side of the bed so that her fingertips rested on the edge of the box.

Lyle looked in and saw Leah's open eyes glinting in the dark. She looked curious and patient. When he touched her perfectly smooth, silky cheek with his finger, her mouth reached toward it, pulling from the side.

He couldn't keep himself from pressing his nose into her cheek and then rubbing it along the soft spot down the middle of her head. He smelled the most unusual, appealing musky smell. It was the baby's smell. That must be what mother horses smelled when they licked their newborns dry and got that anxious, hungry, tone to their voices.

Leah didn't seem to mind as Lyle touched her and held her hand, so he slipped his arm under her neck and down through the warm blanket under her back. He slid her out of the apple box and into his lap. Then he scooted himself against the wall. He felt a rush of wonder.

He snuggled his face into Leah's tiny perfect face again. She made a soft squeaking sound like a tiny newborn puppy might, or a baby bird.

When Winny's hand jarred the apple crate, Lyle looked up. She was watching him, her cheekbone against the edge of the mattress and her eyes glinting in the firelight the way Leah's had been. Her smile was sleepy.

"How is she?" Winny asked, her voice quiet.

"Perfect," Lyle answered.

Sources

Mukkala, Benjamin C. *The Shanty Boys.*

Mull, Carol E. *The Underground Railroad in Michigan.*

Swierenga, Robert P. *The Dutch and the Ottawas: A Unique Cultural Interchange.*

van Reken, Donald L. *The Holland fire of October 8, 1871.*

Donald L. van Reken, "The Railroads of Holland, Michigan." Volume One, The Nineteenth Century.

Notes

"The great theologian" that Dominie VandePol refers to and quotes in chapter 1 is Jonathan Edwards, from the famous sermon, "Sinners in the Hands of an Angry God."

Reverend Albertus C. Van Raalte is a historical figure, both a doctor and reverend, who founded Holland.

The Ottawa referred to by name is Waukazoo, another historical figure who helped the Dutch as they settled Holland.

Acknowledgements

Thank you to Mary (and the late R. Dirk) Jellema, who supported me with a subscription to *Origins* (Historical Magazine of Calvin College and Seminary Archives), and in 100 other ways. Thanks to my Swede, Kenneth, my most faithful reader. Thanks to Jane de Roussan, my editor who sees straight into a story and finds where to shore it up and where to nurture the story line into something bigger. Thanks to my Grandpa Woodard who, sadly, died before I was born, yet none-the-less left me the Arthur Ritis joke. Thanks to my Dutch church and Dutch uncles and cousins who donated their names and their big hearts to my book. It's the Dutch side of the family who gave me their big faith, and the English side (Mother!) that brings a breath of fresh air wherever they appear. And of course, it's my own family's long-ago horses that inspired me to capture them in my stories—Scarlet, Red and Applejack, Satin and King— to keep me company for the journey.

Made in the USA
Middletown, DE
15 September 2022